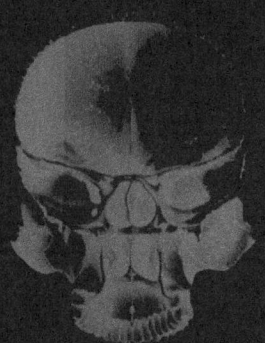

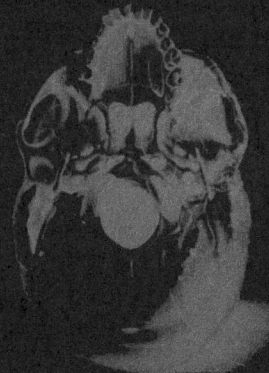

MARTIN CONAGHAN
WILL PICKERING

BURKE
&HARE
THE GRAPHIC NOVEL

BURKE & HARE

Third Edition

© Copyright 2009, 2011, 2017 Martin Conaghan and Will Pickering
All rights reserved

Published by Caliber Comics, a division of Caliber Entertainment LLC.

Apart from any use permitted under International copyright law, this publication may only be reproduced, stored or transmitted, in any form, or by any means, with prior permission in writing of the publishers, or in the case of reprographic production, in accordance with the terms of licences issued by the Copyright Licensing Agency. All character portayals in this publication are fictitious. Any similarity between characters, names and/or institutions, living or dead, is purely coincidental but for purposes of satire or historical representation and should not be inferred.

BURKE & HARE
a true story of medicine, murder and money

This edition is dedicated to Gary Reed.

"When in the guise of fiction an author maligns in the most unmistakable terms the memories of men who have not long departed, he should recollect that someone still may live who can answer to refute his calumnies."

- JAMES GOODSIR *in a letter to the* PALL MALL GAZETTE on ROBERT LOUIS STEVENSON'S *The Body-Snatcher*, 1885.

written by MARTIN CONAGHAN · *illustrated by* WILL PICKERING
lettered by PAUL McLAREN
logo and cover design by RIAN HUGHES at DEVICE
edited by NIC WILKINSON
Publisher ERIC REICHERT

CONTENTS

INTRODUCTION

CHAPTER.	TITLE.
I.	In Which We Meet Mr Burke
II.	A Woman From Gilmerton
III.	The Sale of the Century
IV.	The Lovely Month of May
V.	The Long Road Home
VI.	Ladies For Sale
VII.	A Thing of Rare Beauty
VIII.	In Cold Blood
IX.	For A Sheep As A Lamb
X.	The Butcher, The Thief and the Boy Who Bought The Beef
XI.	To The Last
XII.	The Sleep of The Just
XIII.	The Last of Mister Burke
XIV.	The Last of Mister Black
XV.	The Clearing
XVI.	Letters and Lies
XVII.	Who Will Venture To Pronounce?
XVII.	Onwards to Glasgow
XVIX.	Of Winters Yet to Come

EPILOGUE............ A Final Exchange

APPENDIX

BIBLIOGRAPHY

BONUS GALLERY

CREDITS

INTRODUCTION

There's a moment in life that I savour: that delicious, perplexing instant when you realise that something you've 'known' for years is actually a crock of nonsense. Like discovering there's no Santa Claus. Or realising your parents *can't* read your mind when you think about sex. The Universe ripples like Predator shimmying through the jungle... and when it rights itself, reality has taken on a slightly different hue.

I had just such a mini-epiphany the first time I read Martin Conaghan and Will Pickering's *Burke & Hare*. At school in the 1950s and '60s I was taught almost no Scottish history, and I spent the next 50 years believing Burke and Hare were 'resurrection men', graverobbers who dug up freshly-buried corpses and sold them for cash. It was a revelation to discover they were actually serial killers, vile brutes who measured the price of human life in pounds, shillings and pence, monsters for whom alcohol and smothering were the tools of their trade.

And yet... Burke and Hare were *men*, too. They were human beings who - superficially at least - weren't all that different from their Edinburgh contemporaries. The major difference between them and most of the human race is that they saw murder for financial gain as an acceptable way to earn a living.

Revealing their story in generally short, concise chapters, Martin Conaghan's script is sparing and very much to the point. Indeed, he takes great care not to over-embellish the story with fiction, sticking almost religiously to the facts as presented to us by history. It is an approach which works well, presenting the killers' heart-chilling evil deeds as being almost mundane in their execution.

Will Pickering's art fits the story - and the times - perfectly. Facial expressions are beautifully captured, as are the dress and general atmosphere of the period. The detail on many pages - especially those external shots of Edinburgh in the early 19th Century - is priceless. And Rian Hughes' cover design is exactly what the story inside demands.

Together, Martin and Will have produced something of which they can be very proud. As well as being educational and entertaining, they've gone one better and given us something important.

Hopefully, the Universe will ripple and change for a great many of their readers.

Alan Grant,
Moniaive, July 2009

Chapter One: In Which We Meet Mister Burke.

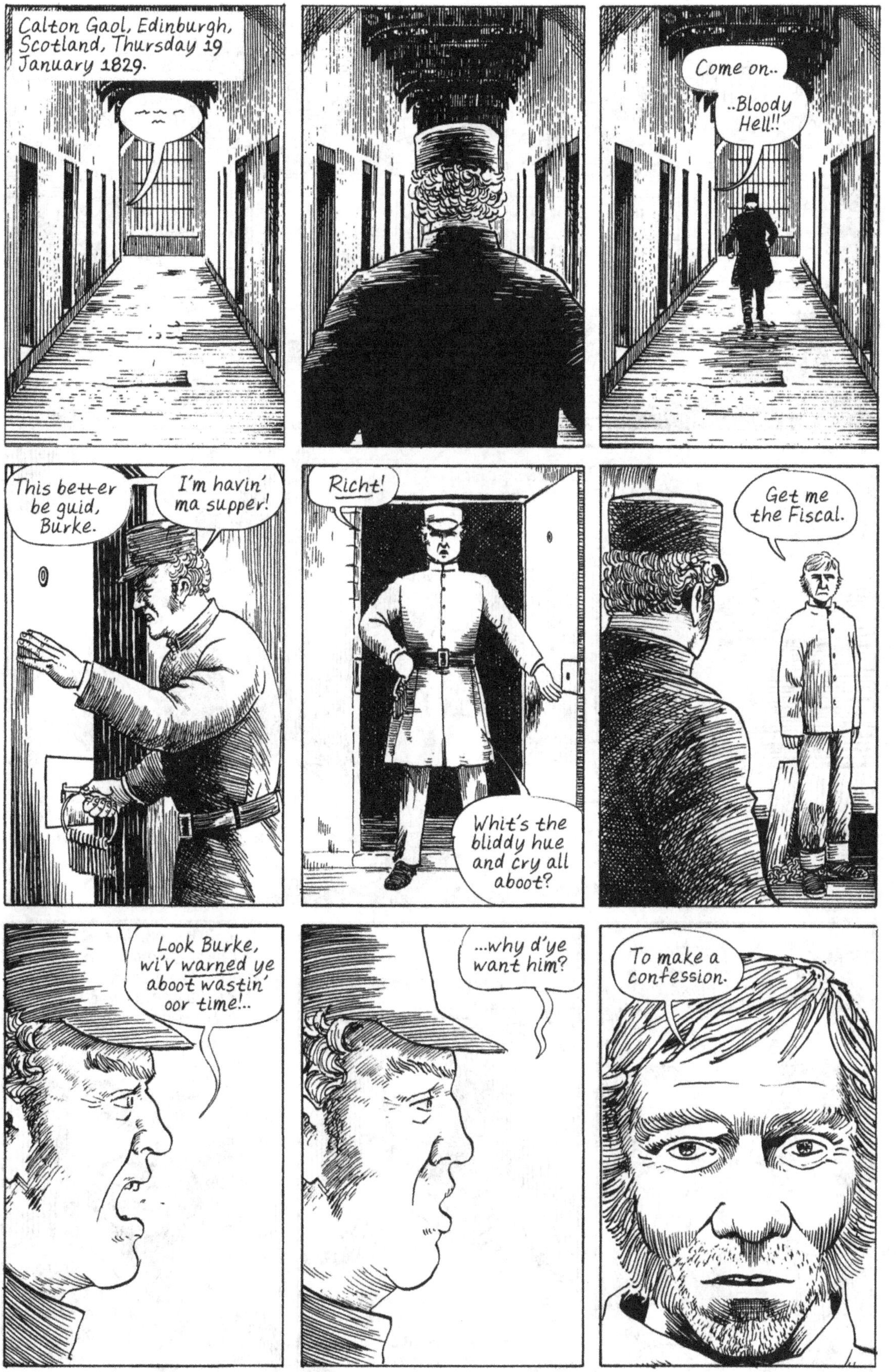

Calton Gaol, Edinburgh, Scotland, Thursday 19 January 1829.
Come on..
..Bloody Hell!!
This better be guid, Burke.
I'm havin' ma supper!
Richt!
Whit's the bliddy hue and cry all aboot?
Get me the Fiscal.
Look Burke, wi'v warned ye aboot wastin' oor time!..
...why d'ye want him?
To make a confession.

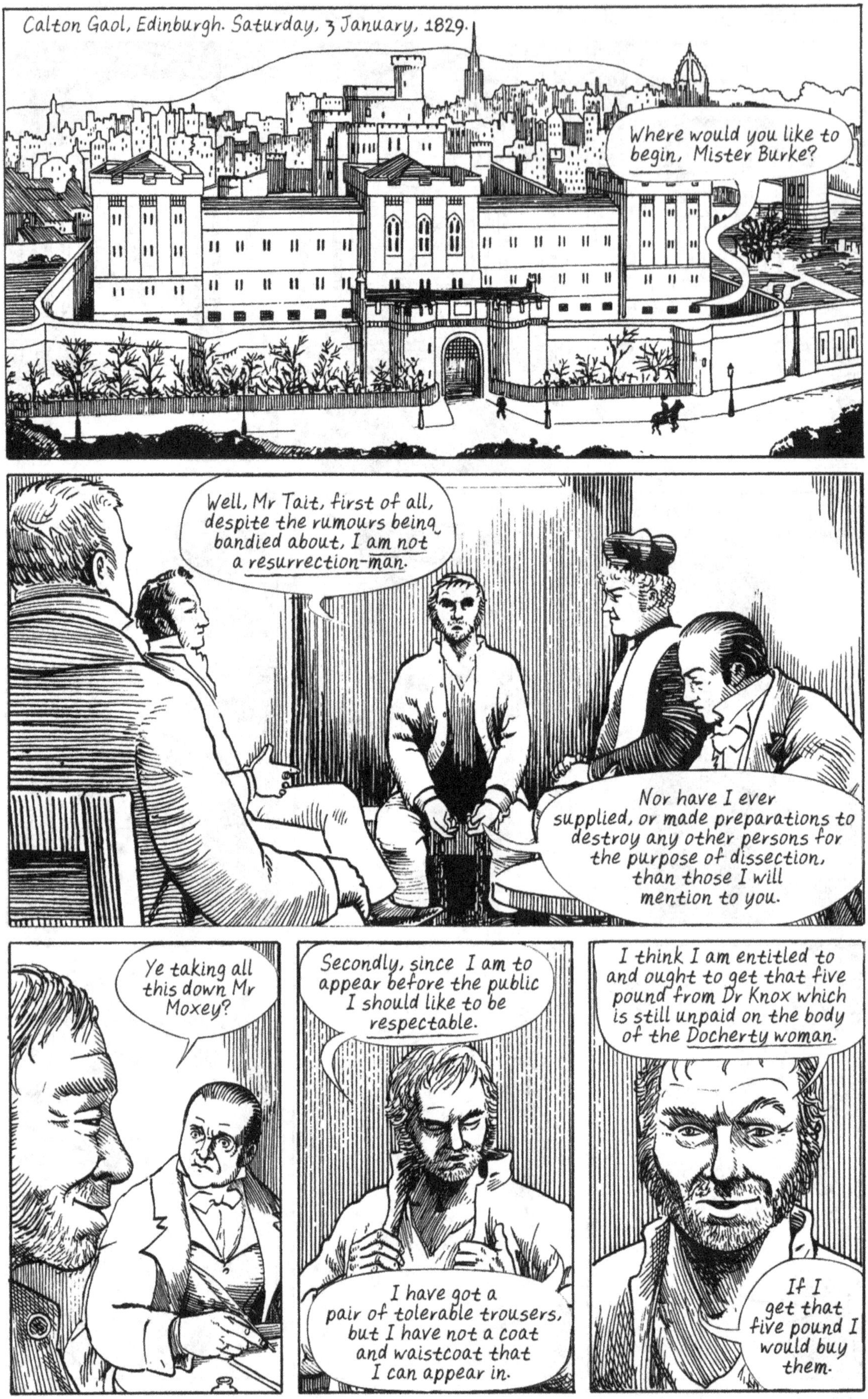
Calton Gaol, Edinburgh. Saturday, 3 January, 1829.
Where would you like to begin, Mister Burke?
Well, Mr Tait, first of all, despite the rumours being bandied about, I am not a resurrection-man.
Nor have I ever supplied, or made preparations to destroy any other persons for the purpose of dissection, than those I will mention to you.
Ye taking all this down Mr Moxey?
Secondly, since I am to appear before the public I should like to be respectable.
I have got a pair of tolerable trousers, but I have not a coat and waistcoat that I can appear in.
I think I am entitled to and ought to get that five pound from Dr Knox which is still unpaid on the body of the Docherty woman.
If I get that five pound I would buy them.

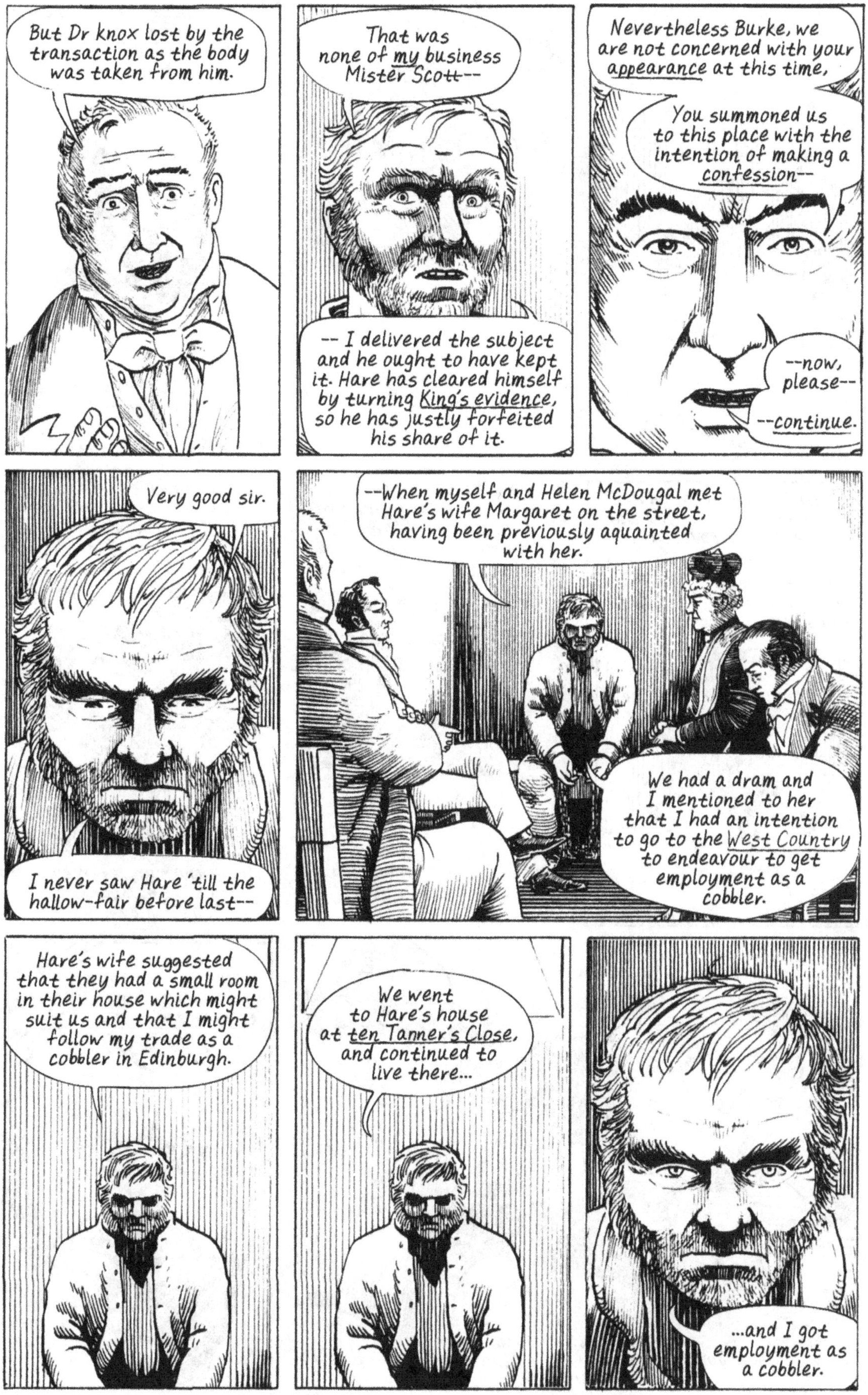
But Dr knox lost by the transaction as the body was taken from him.
That was none of my business Mister Scott--
-- I delivered the subject and he ought to have kept it. Hare has cleared himself by turning King's evidence, so he has justly forfeited his share of it.
Nevertheless Burke, we are not concerned with your appearance at this time,
You summoned us to this place with the intention of making a confession--
--now, please--
--continue.
Very good sir.
I never saw Hare 'till the hallow-fair before last--
--When myself and Helen McDougal met Hare's wife Margaret on the street, having been previously aquainted with her.
We had a dram and I mentioned to her that I had an intention to go to the West Country to endeavour to get employment as a cobbler.
Hare's wife suggested that they had a small room in their house which might suit us and that I might follow my trade as a cobbler in Edinburgh.
We went to Hare's house at ten Tanner's Close, and continued to live there...
...and I got employment as a cobbler.

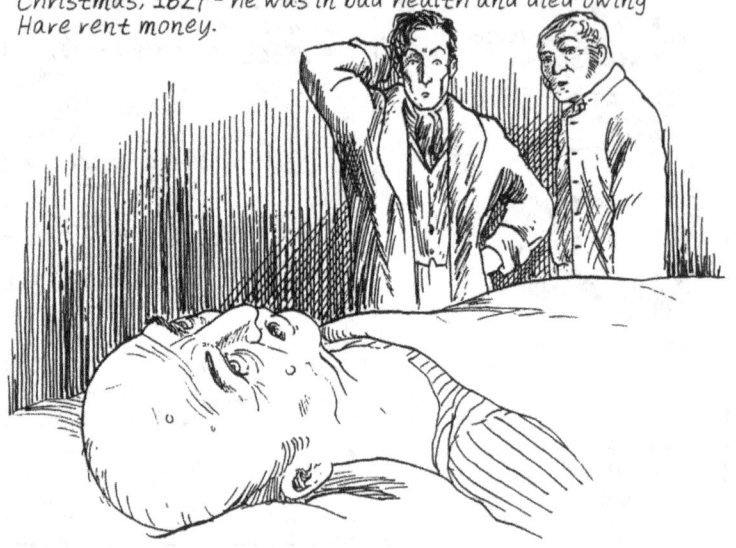

"An old pensioner named Donald lived in the house about Christmas, 1827 – he was in bad health and died owing Hare rent money.

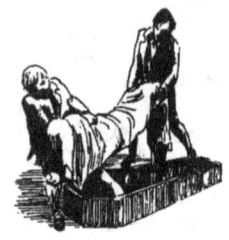

"Hare proposed that his body should be sold to the doctors, and that I should get a share of the price.

"Hare started the lid of Donald's coffin with a chisel and we took out the corpse and hid it in the bed.

We put tanner's bark from behind the house into the coffin and covered it with a sheet.

The coffin was taken away to be buried.

"Since we had never been concerned in anything of the kind before, and were at a loss how to get the body disposed of, we went to the yard of the college.

"We saw a person like a student there and asked him if there were any of Dr Monro's men about.

"The young man asked what we wanted with Dr Monro and I told him that we had a body to dispose of.

"The young man referred us to Dr Knox, at number ten Surgeons' Square.

"There we saw Jones, Miller and Fergusson – and we disposed of the body for seven pounds and ten shillings."

Dr Knox examined the body and ordered Jones to settle with us.

But he did not ask how we had come by it...

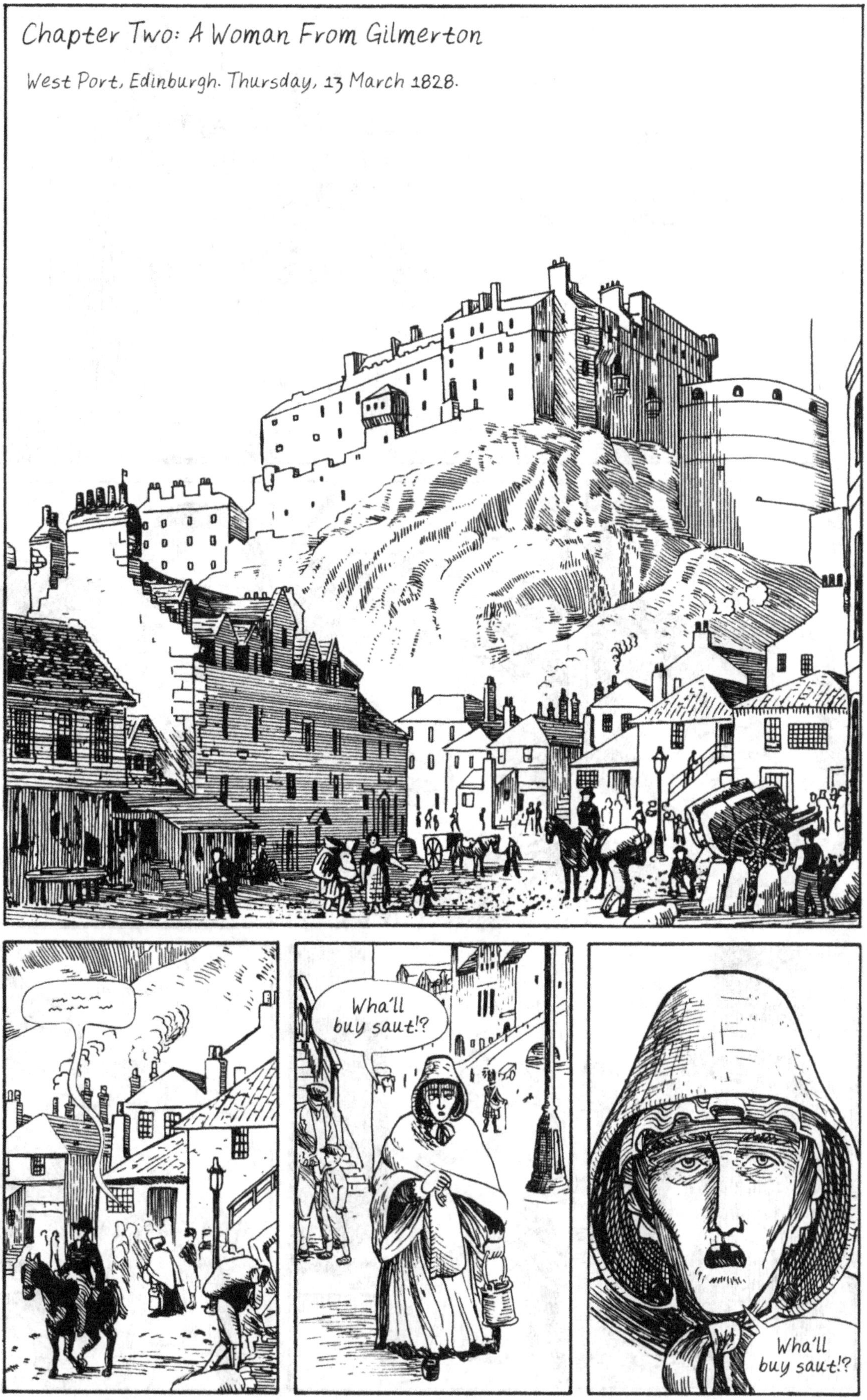
Chapter Two: A Woman From Gilmerton
West Port, Edinburgh. Thursday, 13 March 1828.
Wha'll buy saut!?
Wha'll buy saut!?

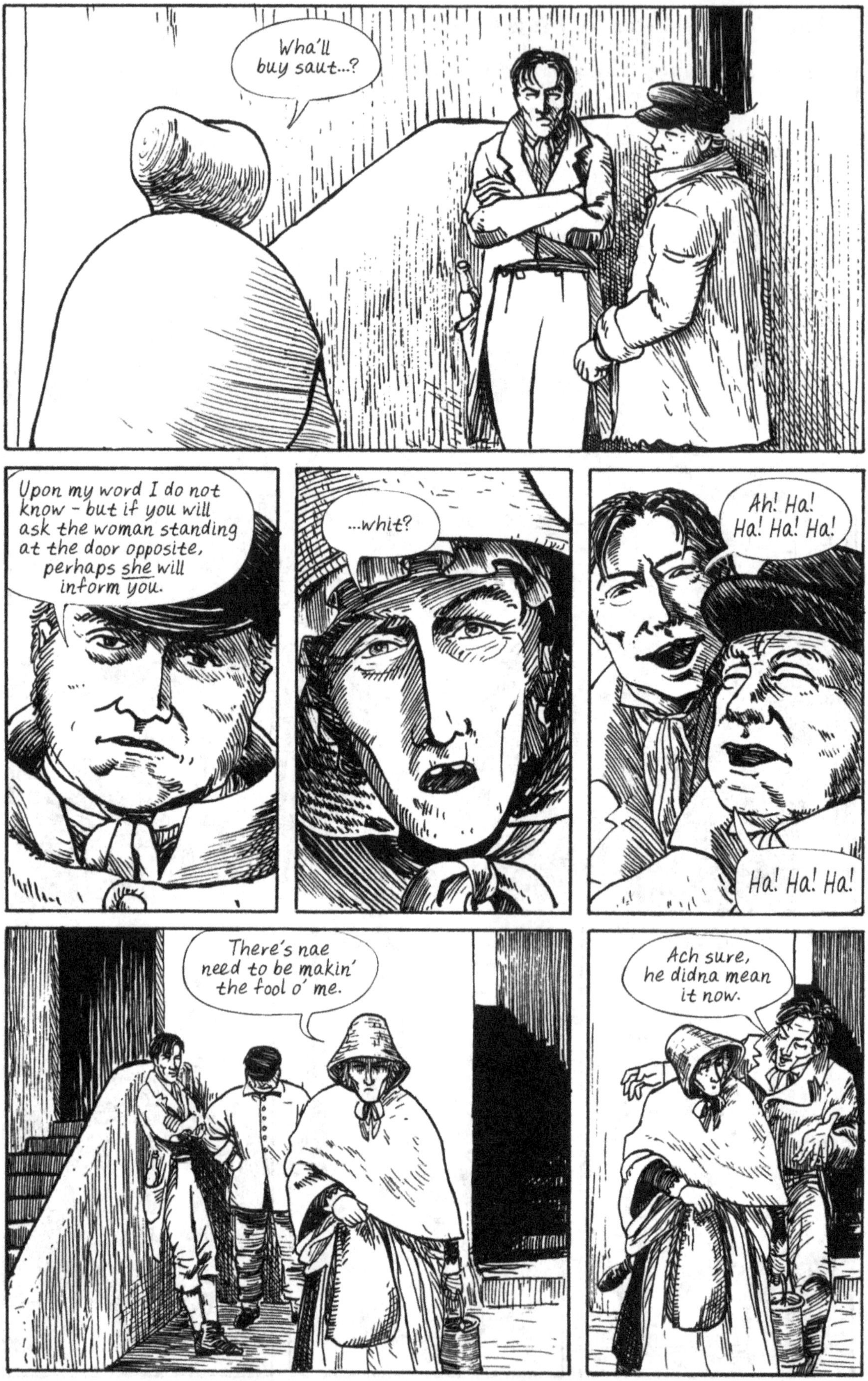
Wha'll buy saut...?
Upon my word I do not know - but if you will ask the woman standing at the door opposite, perhaps she will inform you.
...whit?
Ah! Ha! Ha! Ha! Ha!
Ha! Ha! Ha!
There's nae need to be makin' the fool o' me.
Ach sure, he didna mean it now.

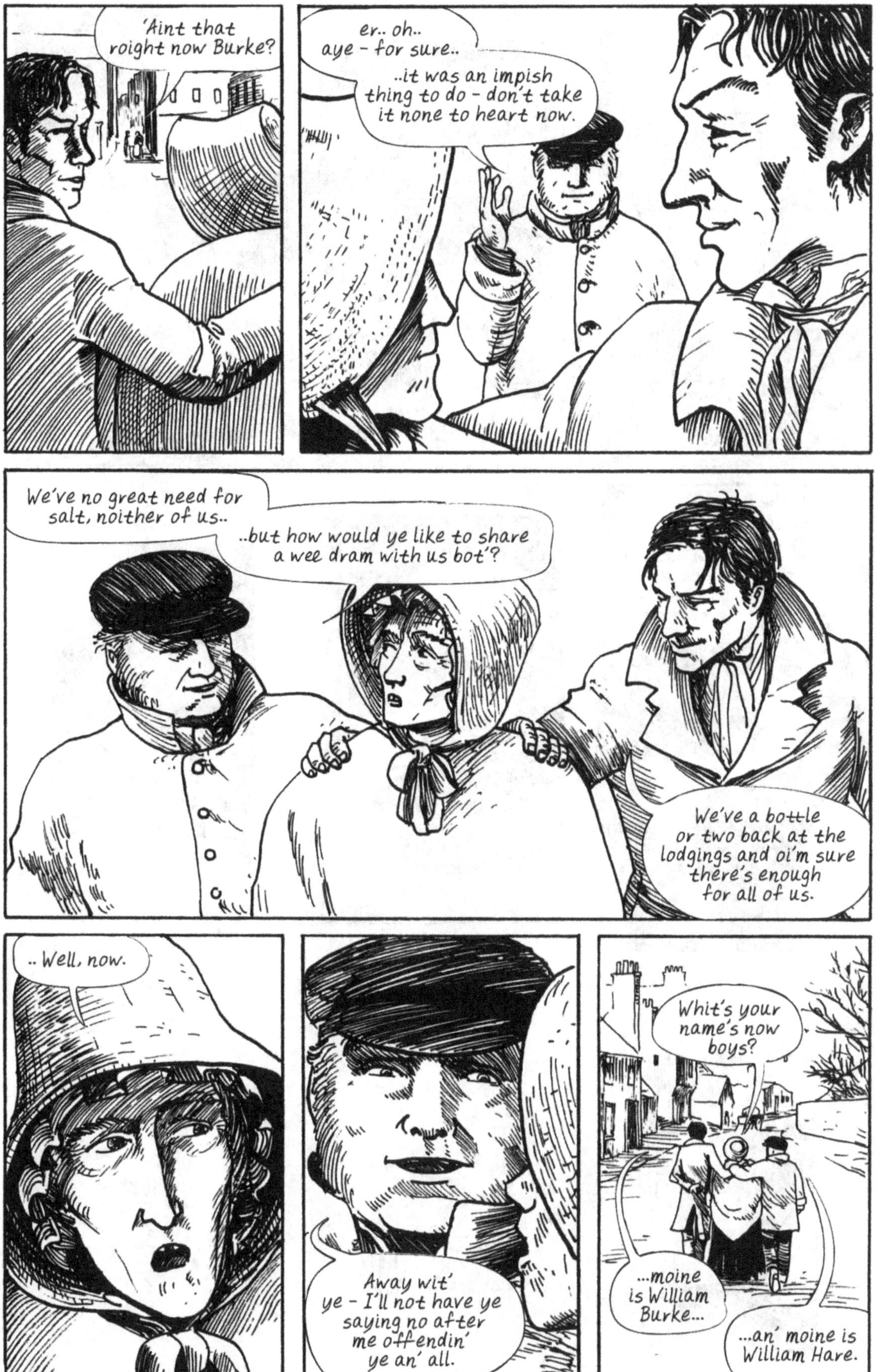

'Aint that roight now Burke?
er.. oh.. aye - for sure..
..it was an impish thing to do - don't take it none to heart now.
We've no great need for salt, noither of us..
..but how would ye like to share a wee dram with us bot'?
We've a bottle or two back at the lodgings and oi'm sure there's enough for all of us.
.. Well, now.
Away wit' ye - I'll not have ye saying no after me offendin' ye an' all.
Whit's your name's now boys?
...moine is William Burke...
...an' moine is William Hare.

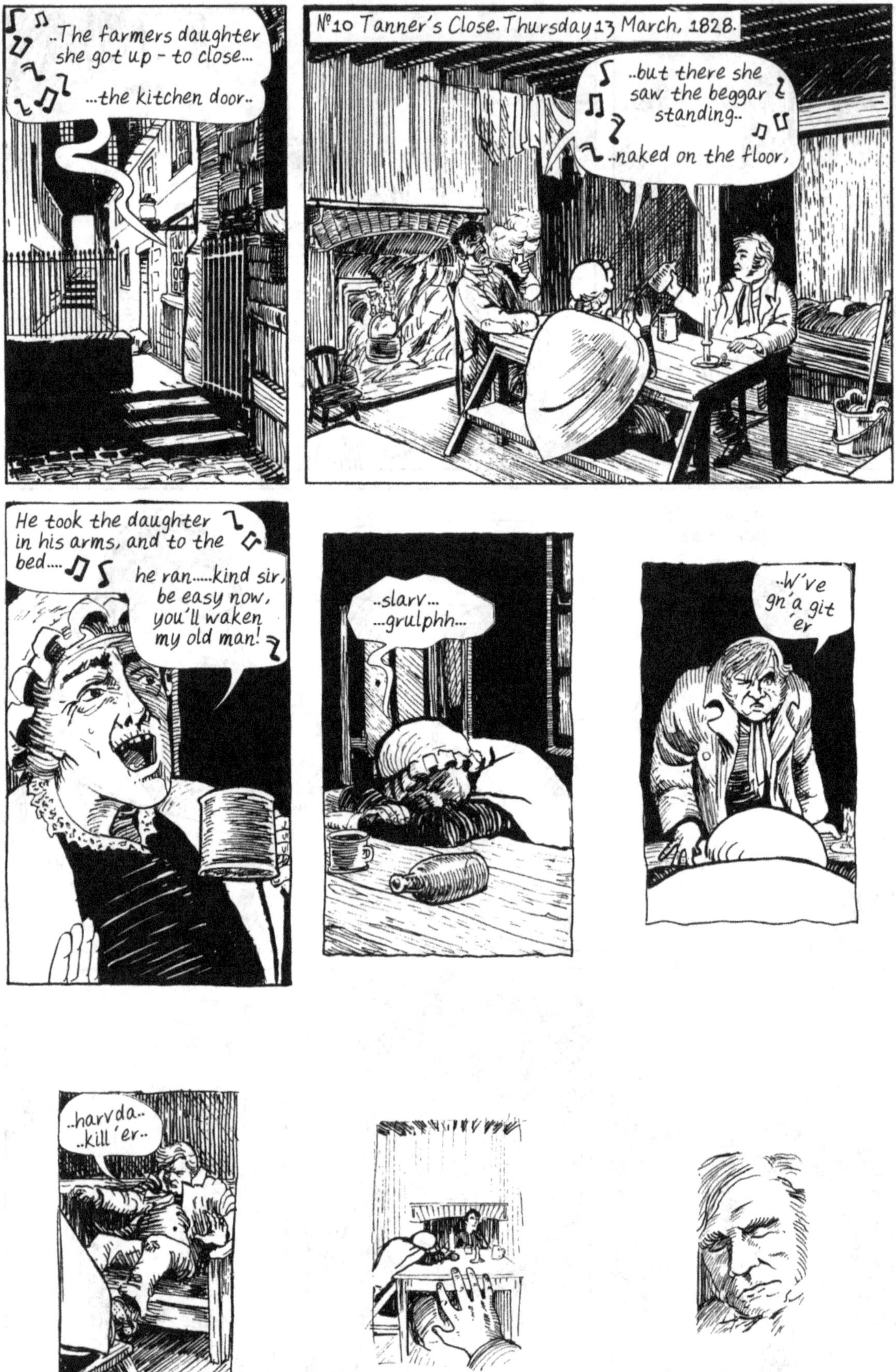
..The farmers daughter she got up - to close...
...the kitchen door..
№10 Tanner's Close. Thursday 13 March, 1828.
..but there she saw the beggar standing..
..naked on the floor,
He took the daughter in his arms, and to the bed....
he ran.....kind sir, be easy now, you'll waken my old man!
..slarv...
...grulphh...
..W've gn'a git 'er
..harvda..
..kill 'er..

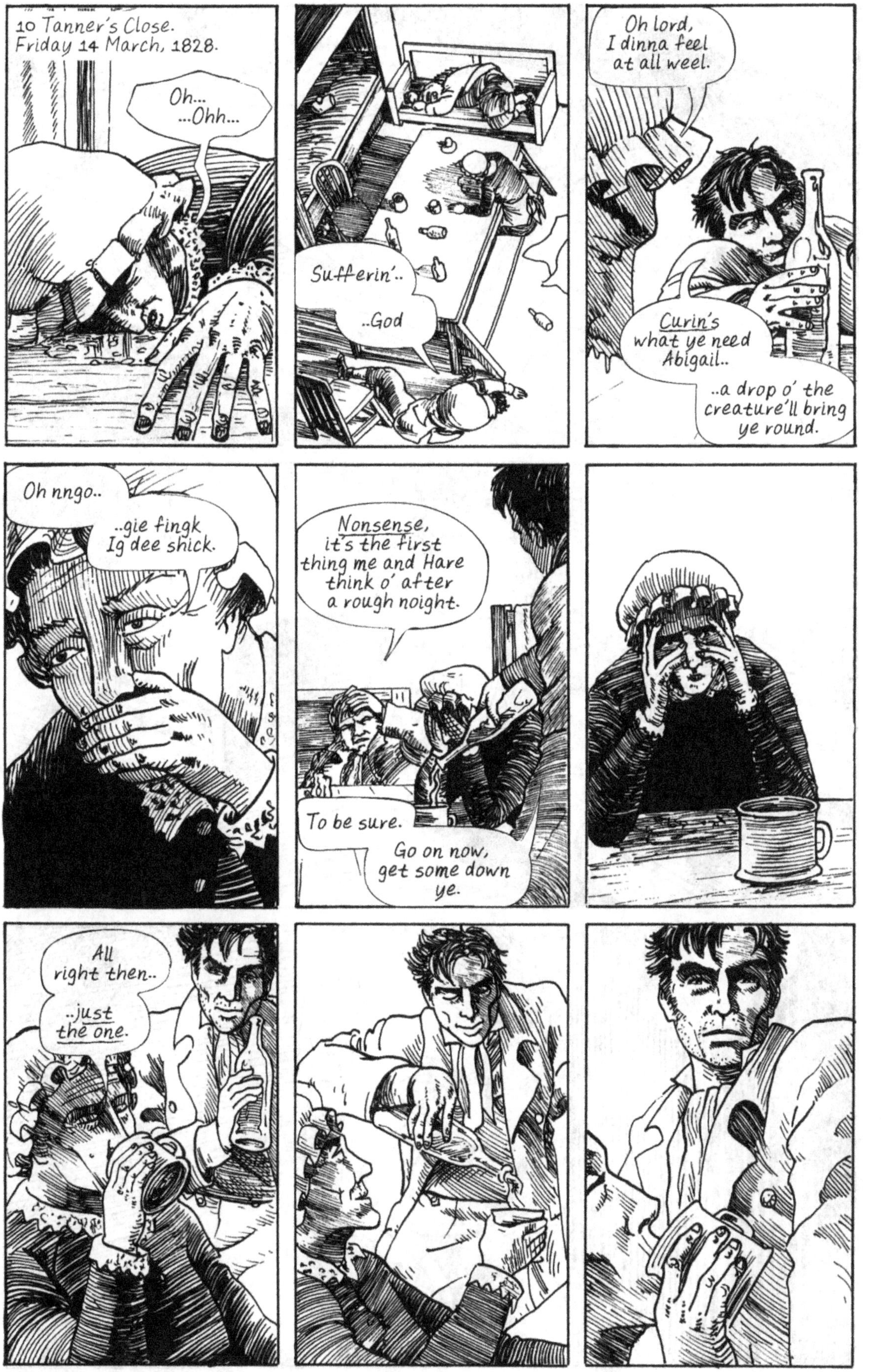
10 Tanner's Close.
Friday 14 March, 1828.
Oh... ...Ohh...
Sufferin'..
..God
Oh lord, I dinna feel at all weel.
Curin's what ye need Abigail..
..a drop o' the creature'll bring ye round.
Oh nngo..
..gie fingk Ig dee shick.
Nonsense, it's the first thing me and Hare think o' after a rough noight.
To be sure.
Go on now, get some down ye.
All right then..
..just the one.

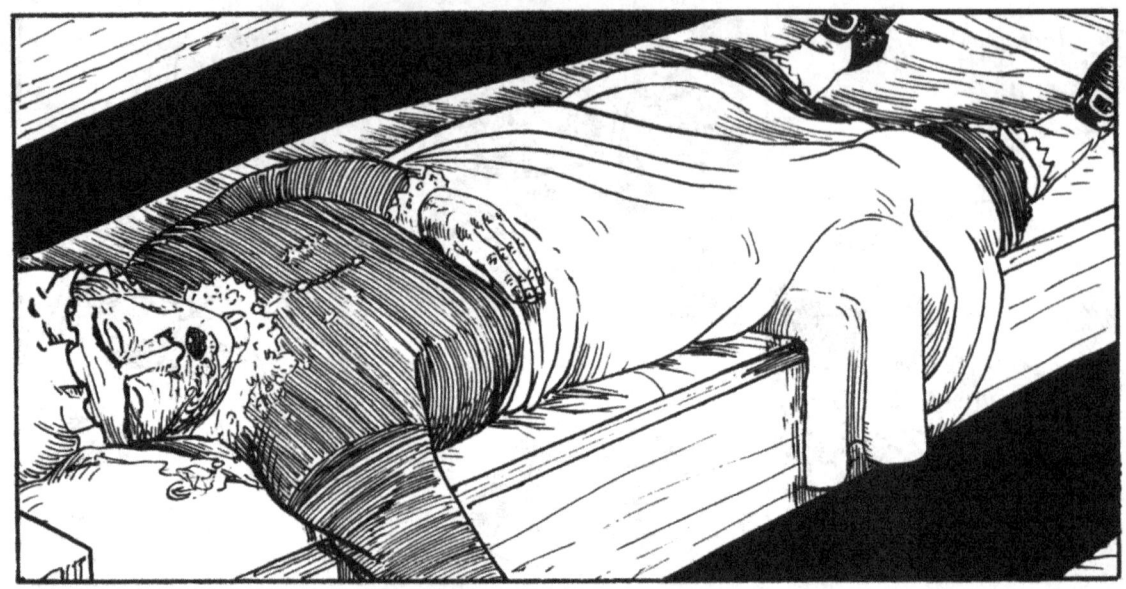

right....

...now...

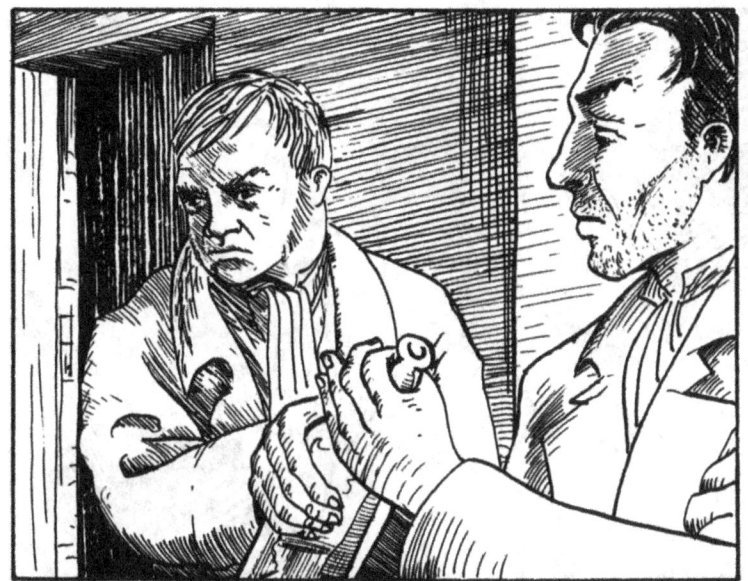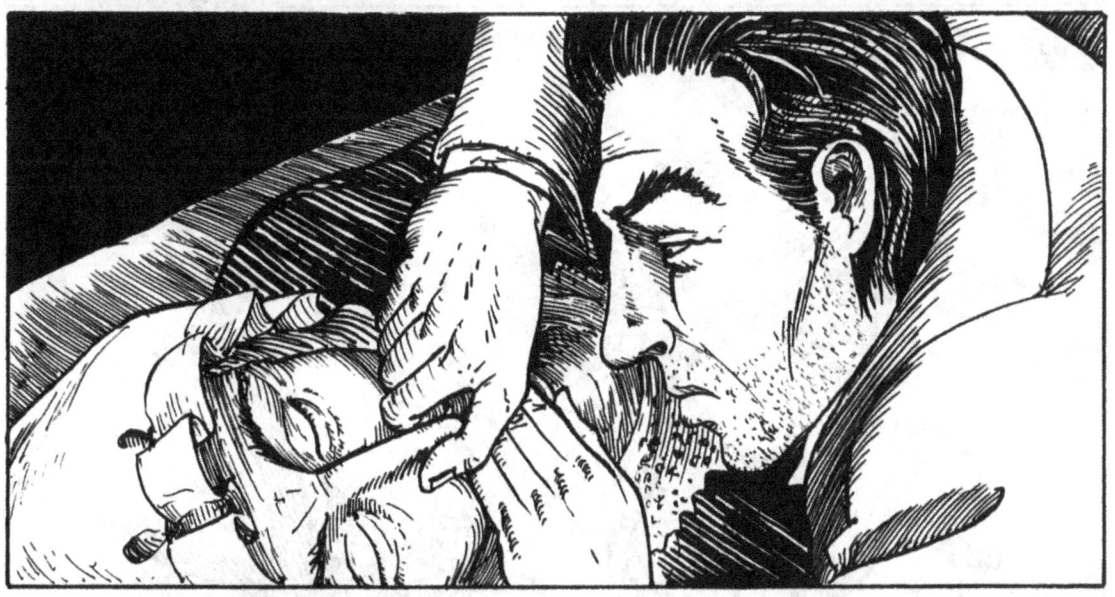

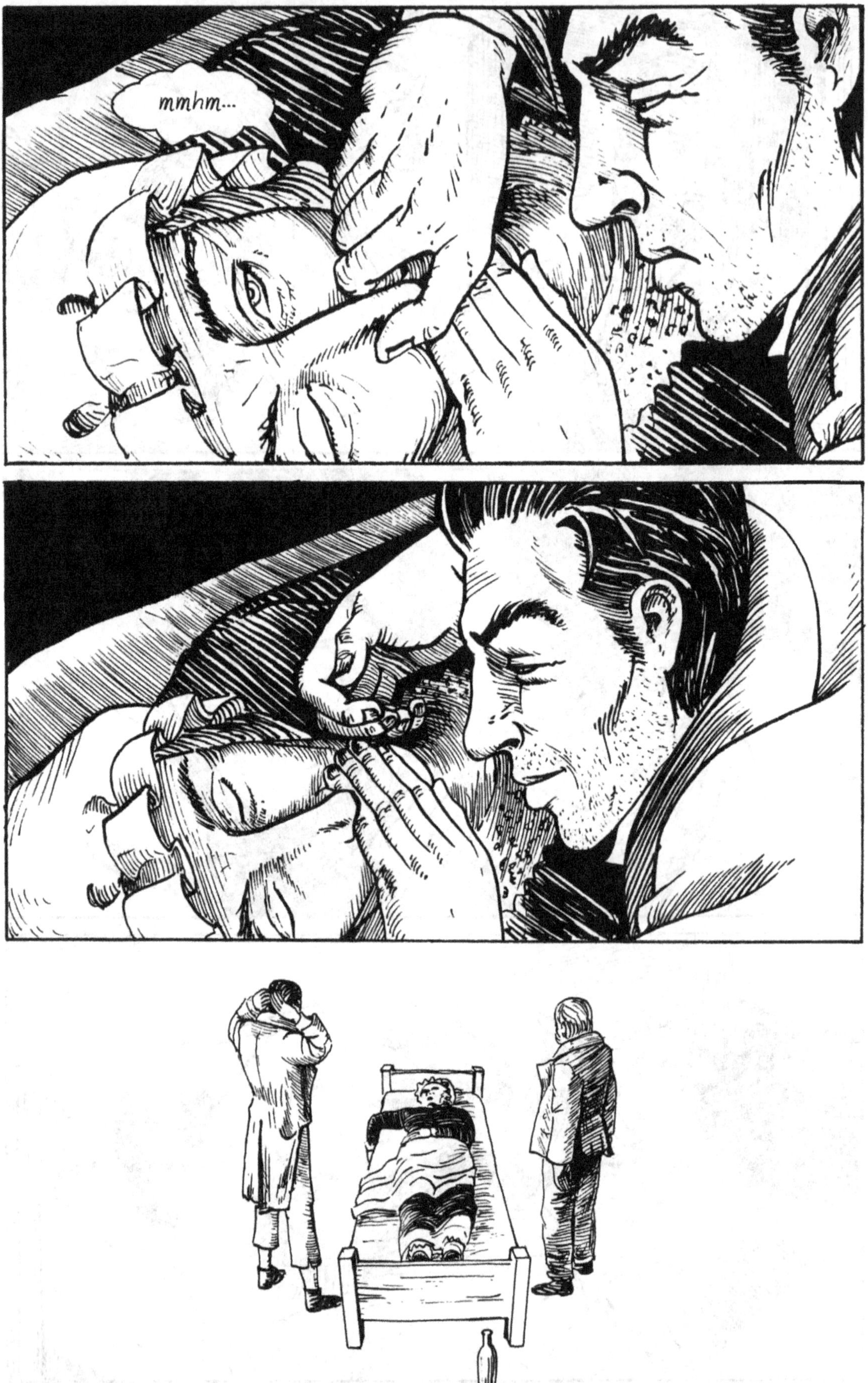
mmhm...

Chapter Three: The Sale of the Century

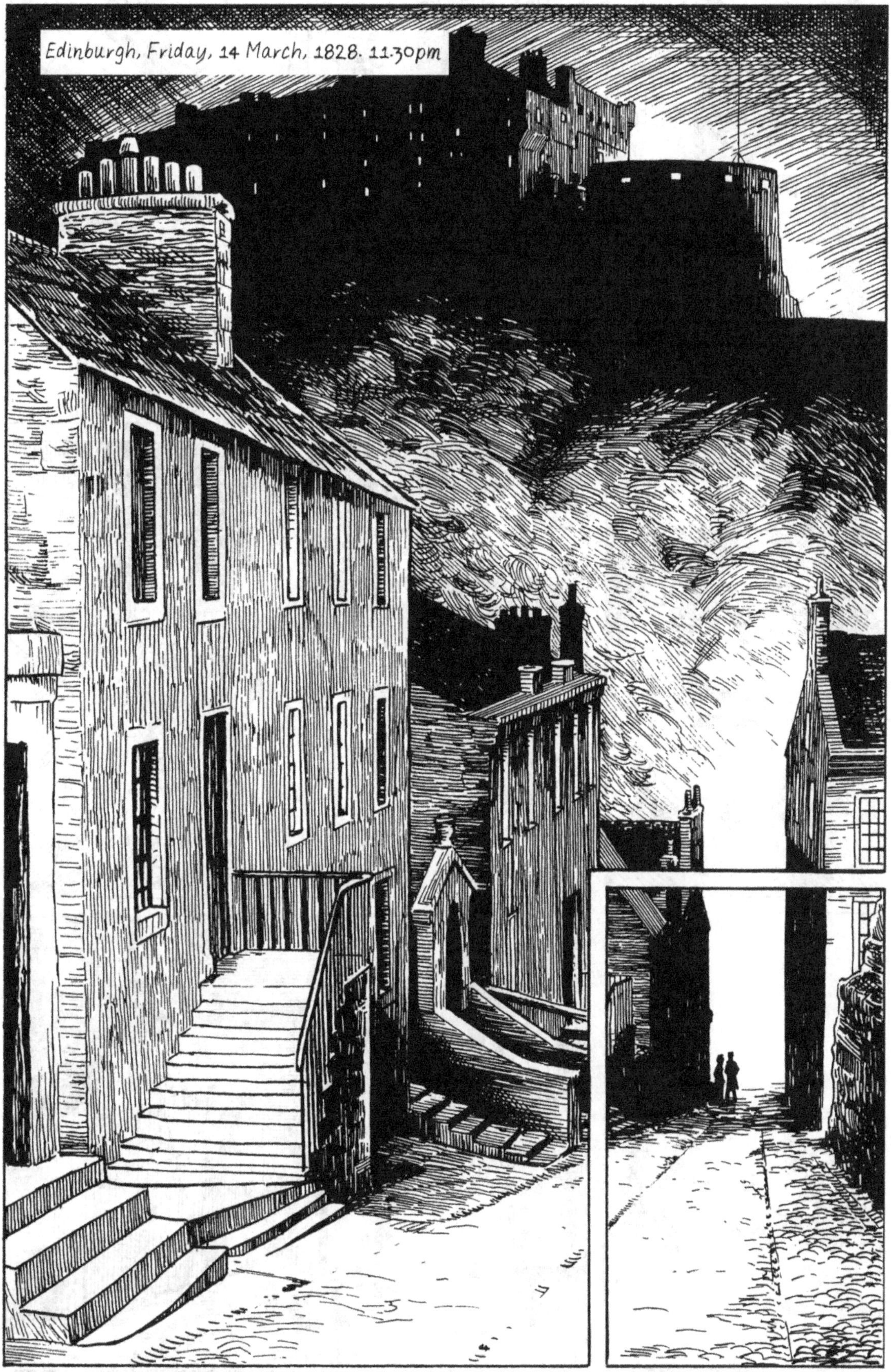
Edinburgh, Friday, 14 March, 1828. 11:30pm

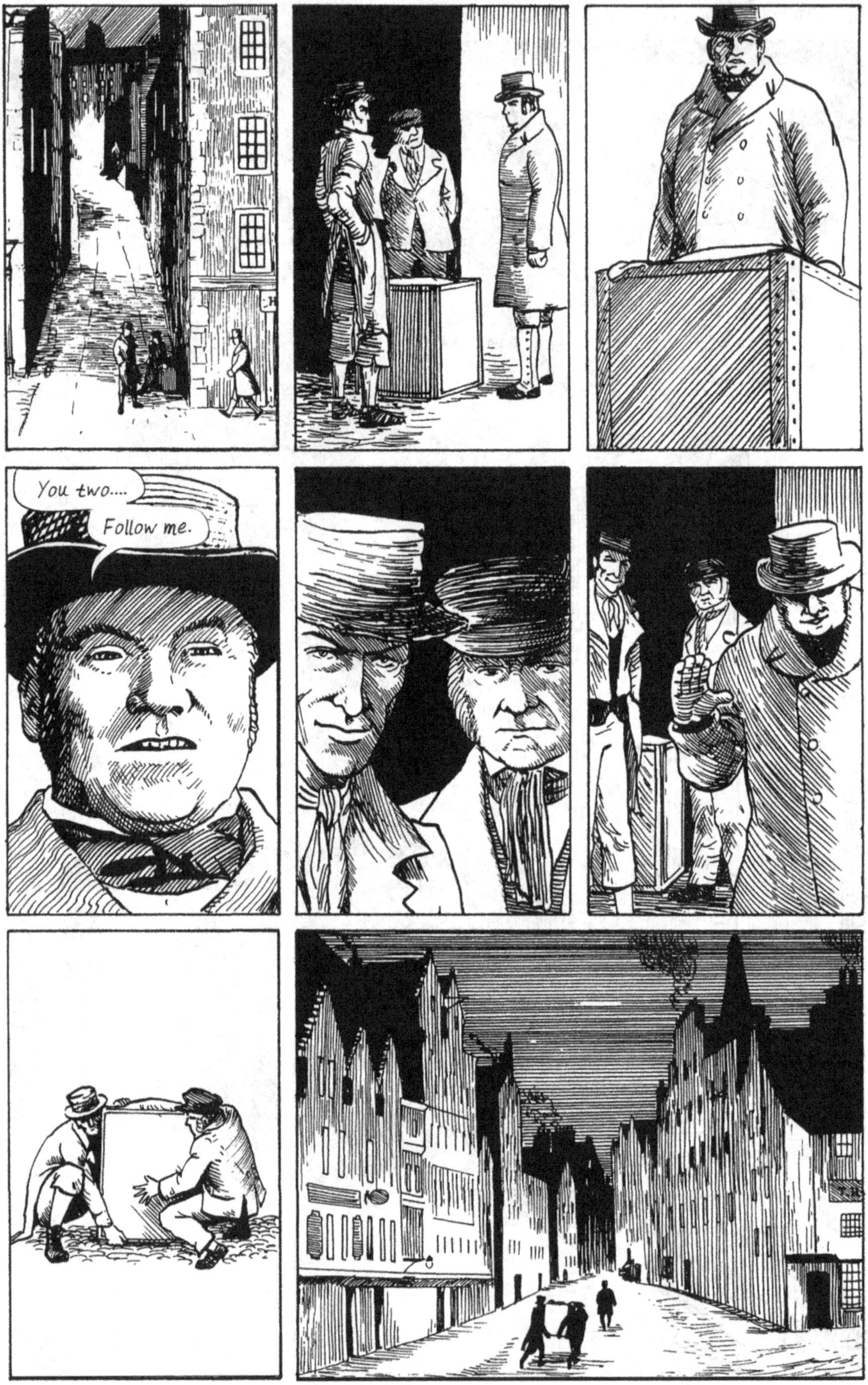
You two....
Follow me.

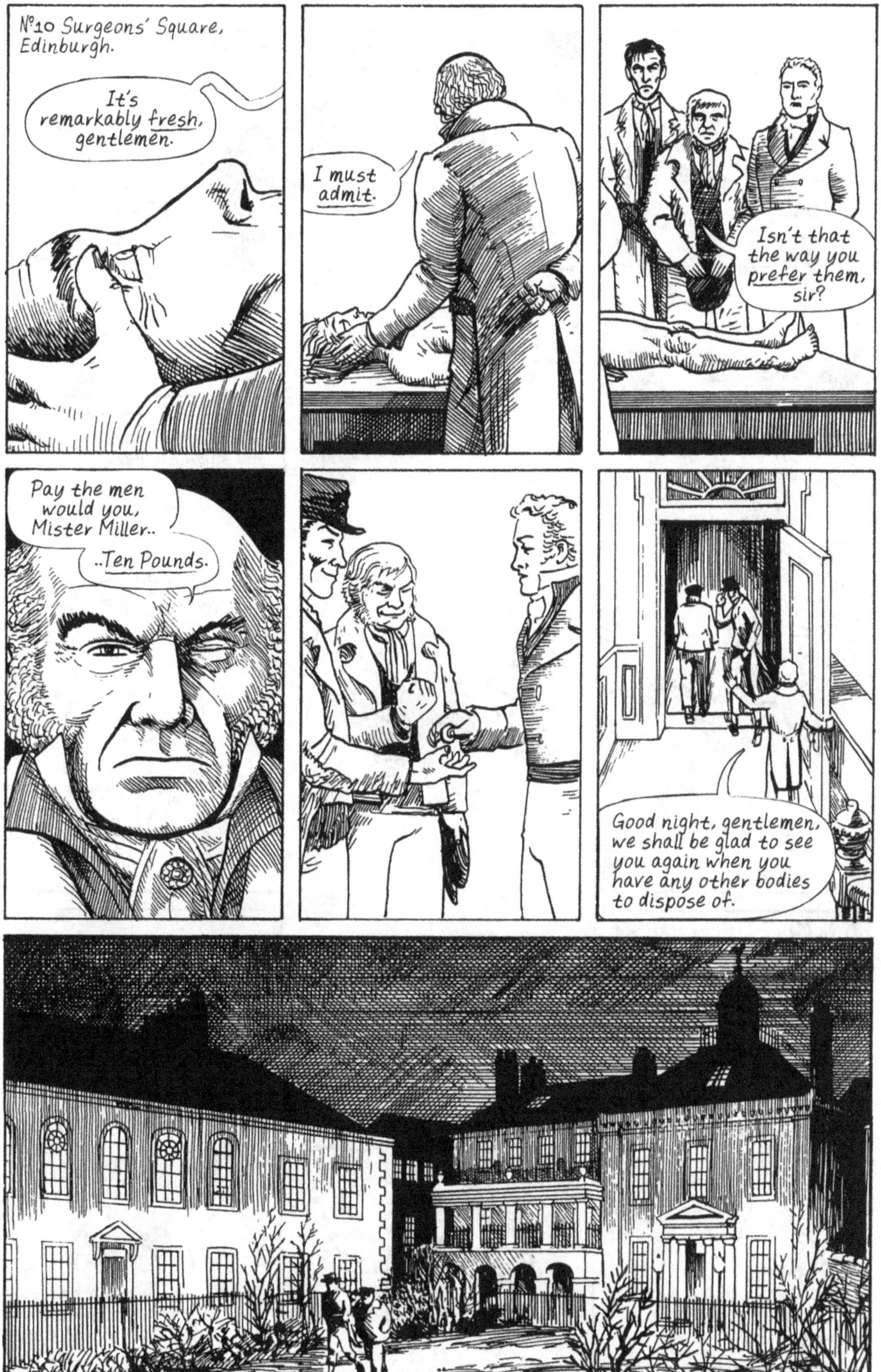

№10 Surgeons' Square, Edinburgh.
It's remarkably fresh, gentlemen.
I must admit.
Isn't that the way you prefer them, sir?
Pay the men would you, Mister Miller..
..Ten Pounds.
Good night, gentlemen, we shall be glad to see you again when you have any other bodies to dispose of.

Chapter Four: The Lovely Month of May

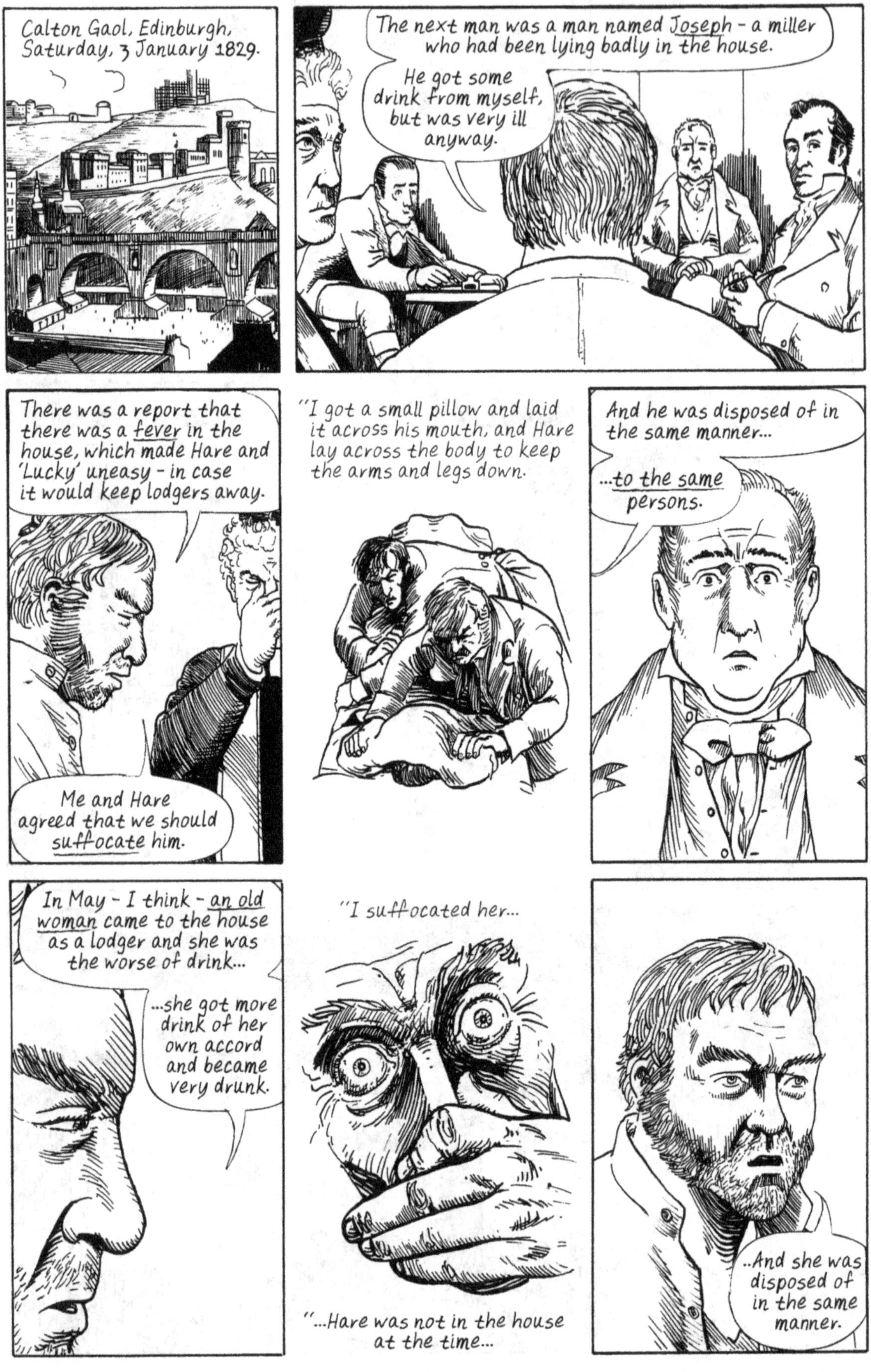

Calton Gaol, Edinburgh, Saturday, 3 January 1829.
The next man was a man named Joseph - a miller who had been lying badly in the house.
He got some drink from myself, but was very ill anyway.
There was a report that there was a fever in the house, which made Hare and 'Lucky' uneasy - in case it would keep lodgers away.
Me and Hare agreed that we should suffocate him.
"I got a small pillow and laid it across his mouth, and Hare lay across the body to keep the arms and legs down.
And he was disposed of in the same manner...
...to the same persons.
In May - I think - an old woman came to the house as a lodger and she was the worse of drink...
...she got more drink of her own accord and became very drunk.
"I suffocated her...
"...Hare was not in the house at the time...
..And she was disposed of in the same manner.

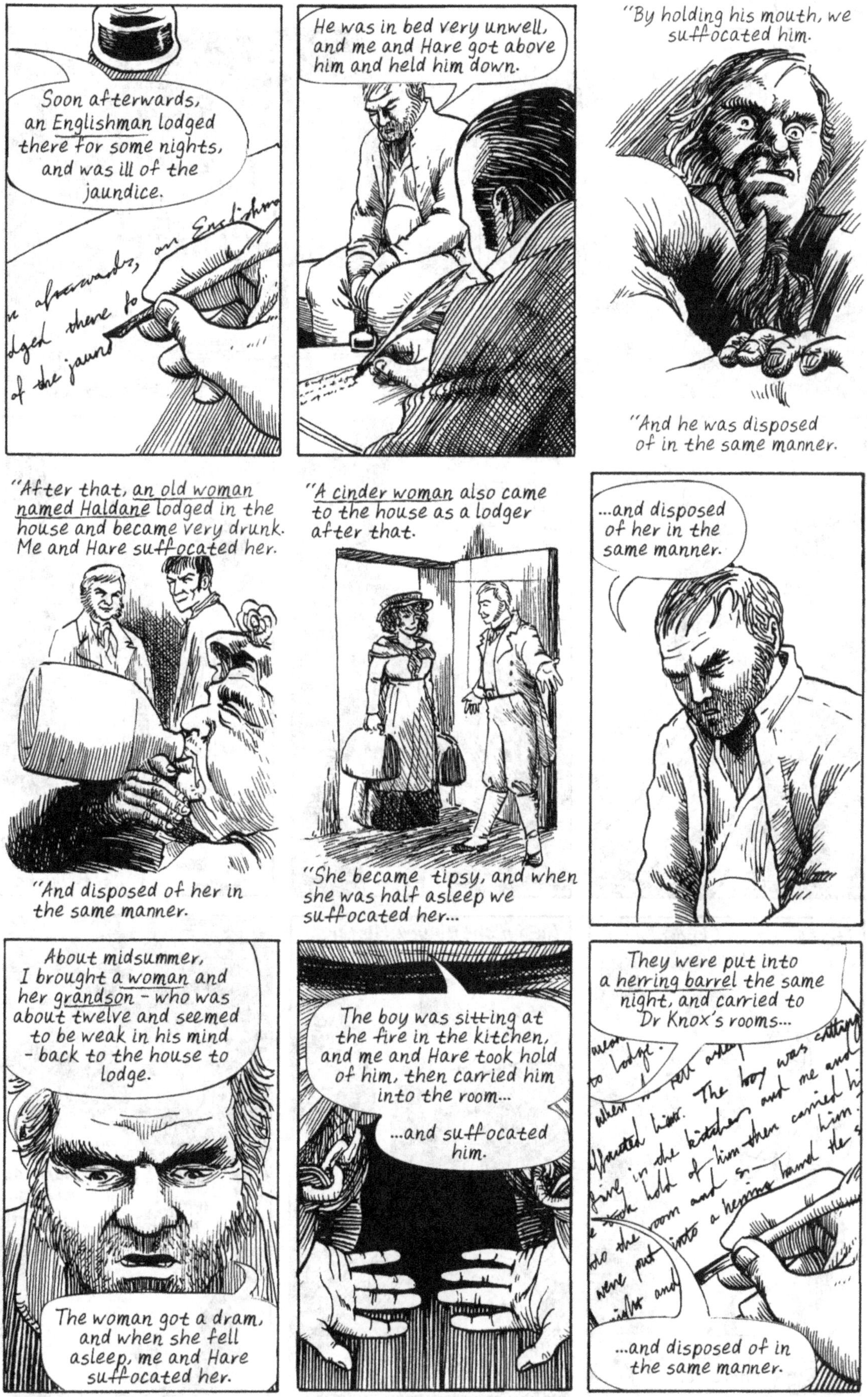
Soon afterwards, an Englishman lodged there for some nights, and was ill of the jaundice.
He was in bed very unwell, and me and Hare got above him and held him down.
"By holding his mouth, we suffocated him.
"And he was disposed of in the same manner.
"After that, an old woman named Haldane lodged in the house and became very drunk. Me and Hare suffocated her.
"And disposed of her in the same manner.
"A cinder woman also came to the house as a lodger after that.
"She became tipsy, and when she was half asleep we suffocated her...
...and disposed of her in the same manner.
About midsummer, I brought a woman and her grandson - who was about twelve and seemed to be weak in his mind - back to the house to lodge.
The woman got a dram, and when she fell asleep, me and Hare suffocated her.
The boy was sitting at the fire in the kitchen, and me and Hare took hold of him, then carried him into the room...
...and suffocated him.
They were put into a herring barrel the same night, and carried to Dr Knox's rooms...
...and disposed of in the same manner.

Chapter Five: The Long Road Home

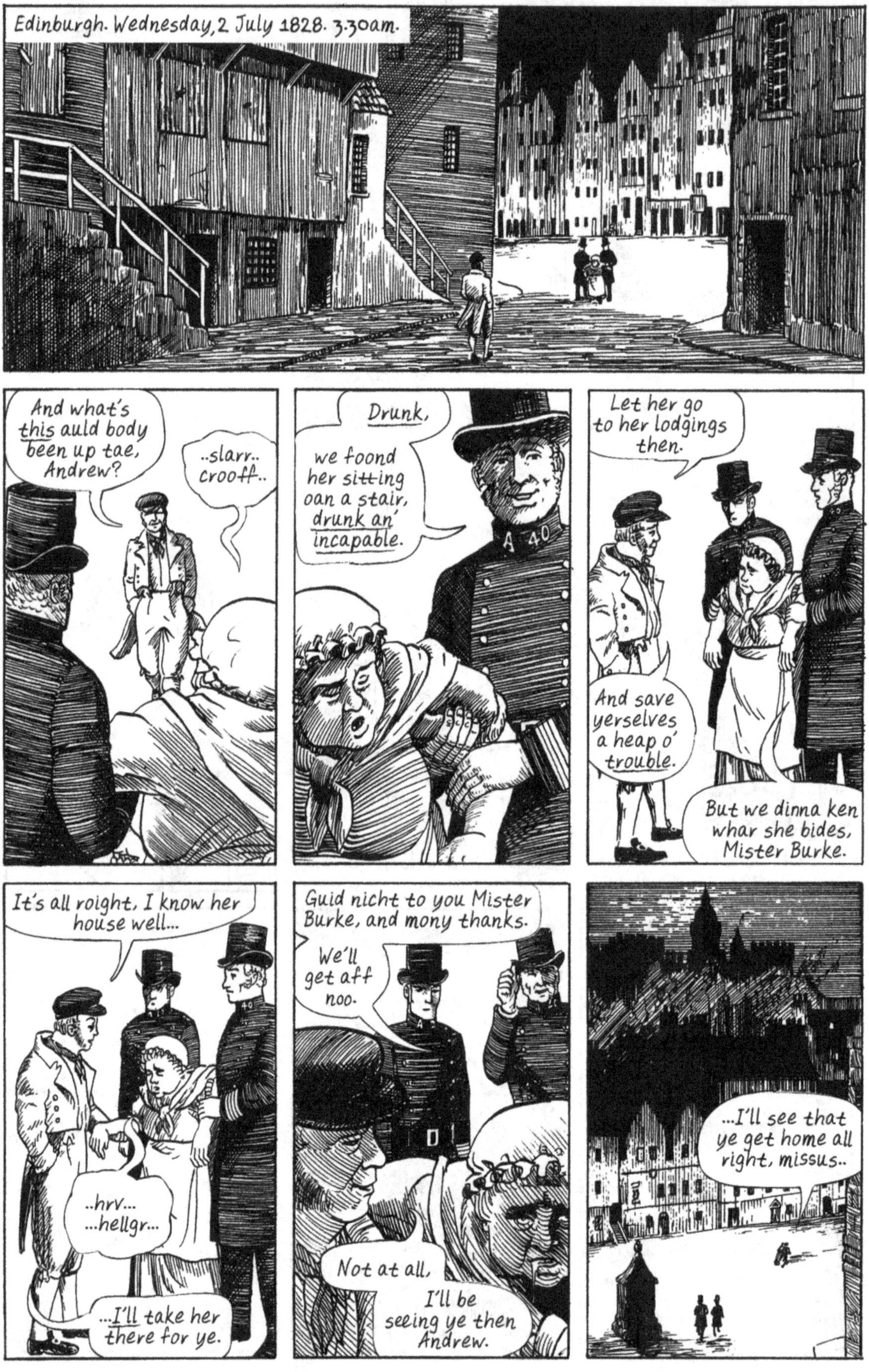
Edinburgh. Wednesday, 2 July 1828. 3.30am.
And what's this auld body been up tae, Andrew?
..slarr.. crooff..
Drunk,
we foond her sitting oan a stair, drunk an' incapable.
Let her go to her lodgings then.
And save yerselves a heap o' trouble.
But we dinna ken whar she bides, Mister Burke.
It's all roight, I know her house well...
..hrv... ...hellgr...
...I'll take her there for ye.
Guid nicht to you Mister Burke, and mony thanks.
We'll get aff noo.
Not at all,
I'll be seeing ye then Andrew.
...I'll see that ye get home all right, missus..

Chapter Six: Ladies For Sale

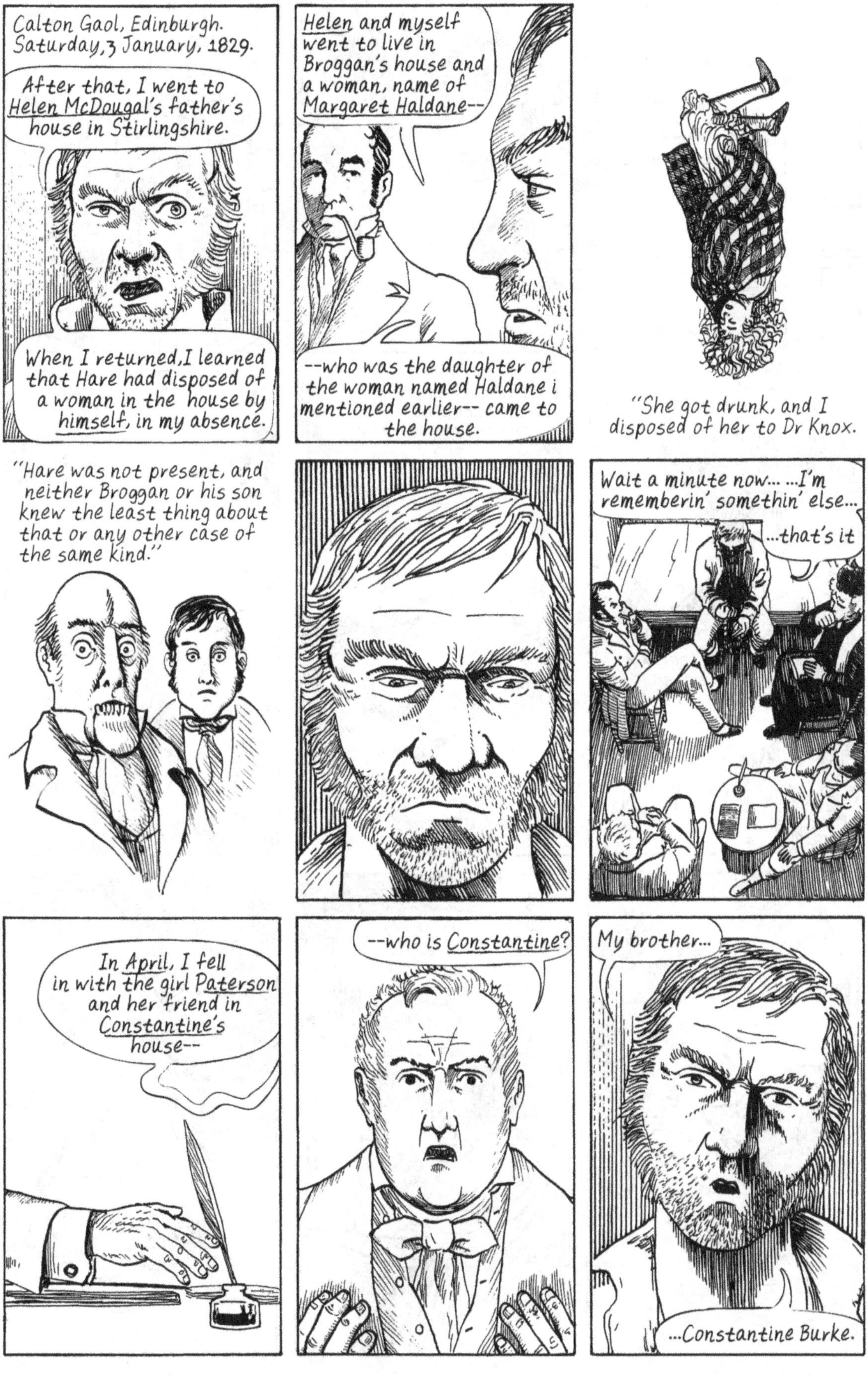

Calton Gaol, Edinburgh. Saturday, 3 January, 1829.
After that, I went to Helen McDougal's father's house in Stirlingshire.
When I returned, I learned that Hare had disposed of a woman in the house by himself, in my absence.
Helen and myself went to live in Broggan's house and a woman, name of Margaret Haldane--
--who was the daughter of the woman named Haldane i mentioned earlier-- came to the house.
"She got drunk, and I disposed of her to Dr Knox.
"Hare was not present, and neither Broggan or his son knew the least thing about that or any other case of the same kind."
Wait a minute now... ...I'm rememberin' somethin' else...
...that's it
In April, I fell in with the girl Paterson and her friend in Constantine's house--
--who is Constantine?
My brother...
...Constantine Burke.

Chapter seven: A Thing of Rare Beauty

Swanston's shop,
Canongate.
Wednesday, 9 April, 1828.

I make about seven pounds a month from me pension.

And I could keep a young lass like you comfortable for the rest of yer life.

So how's about it, why don't ye come back with me and we'll have some breakfast and a few drams at my lodgings?

Come oan Mary, he's just givin' us the patter.

Ye've plenty o' money then, have ye Mister Burke?

To be sure, here—

Billy!...
..git these two lovely ladies a bottle each!

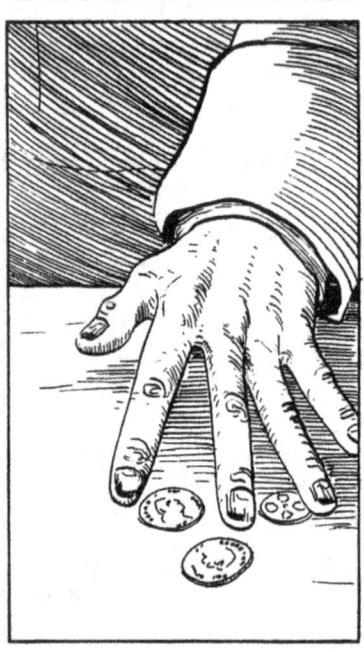

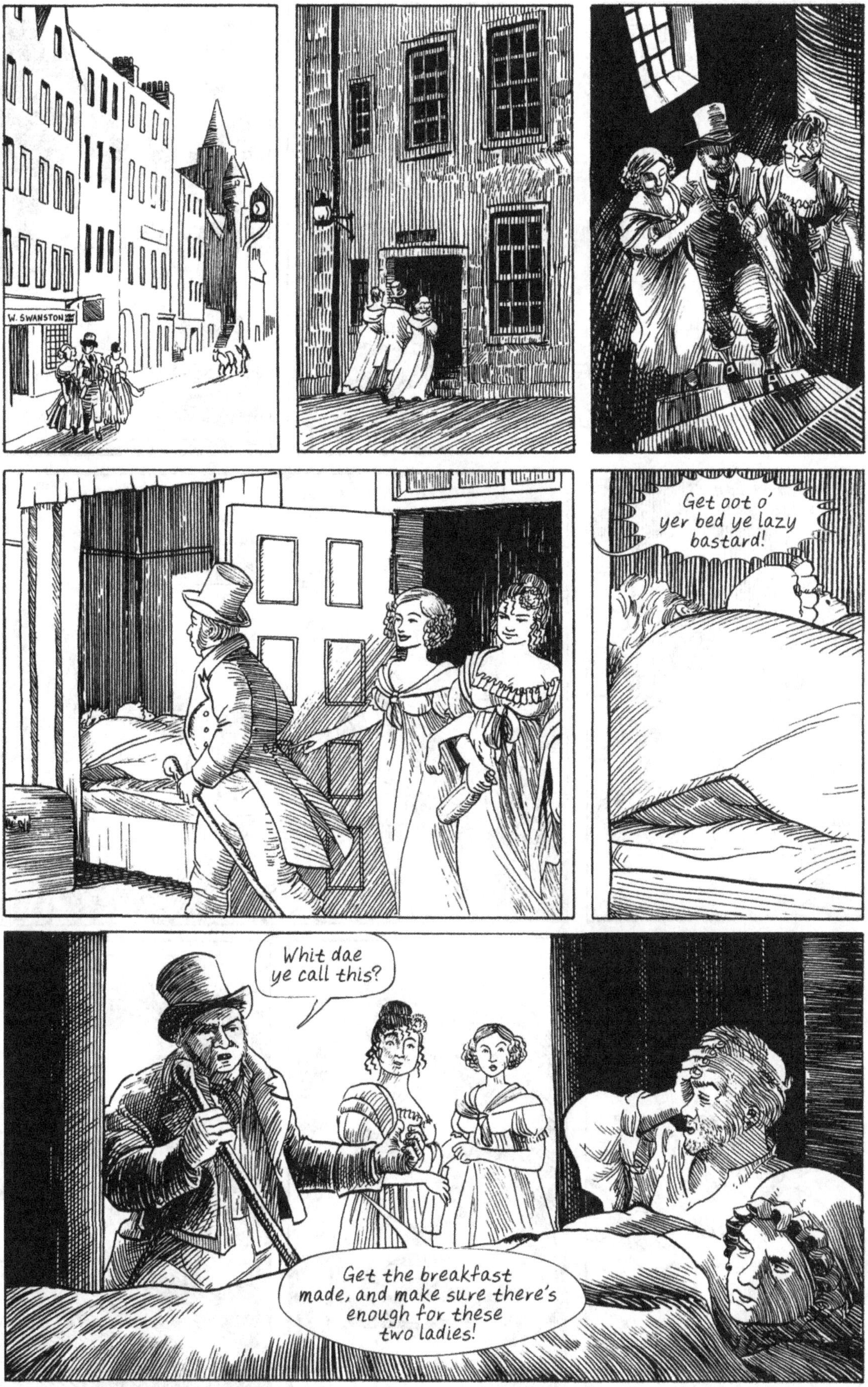
W. SWANSTON
Get oot o' yer bed ye lazy bastard!
Whit dae ye call this?
Get the breakfast made, and make sure there's enough for these two ladies!

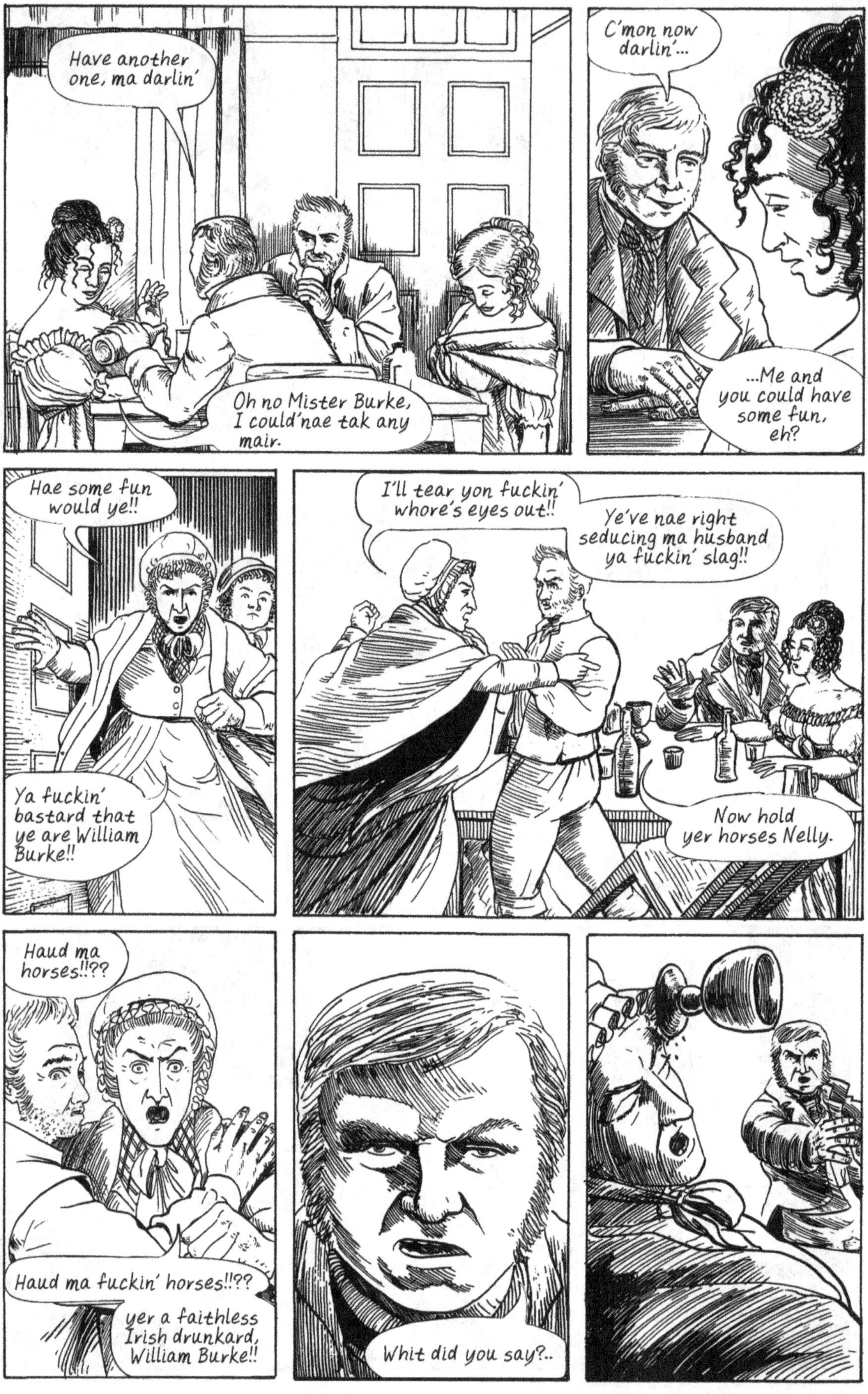
Have another one, ma darlin'
Oh no Mister Burke, I could'nae tak any mair.
C'mon now darlin'...
...Me and you could have some fun, eh?
Hae some fun would ye!!
Ya fuckin' bastard that ye are William Burke!!
I'll tear yon fuckin' whore's eyes out!!
Ye've nae right seducing ma husband ya fuckin' slag!!
Now hold yer horses Nelly.
Haud ma horses!!??
Haud ma fuckin' horses!!??
yer a faithless Irish drunkard, William Burke!!
Whit did you say?..

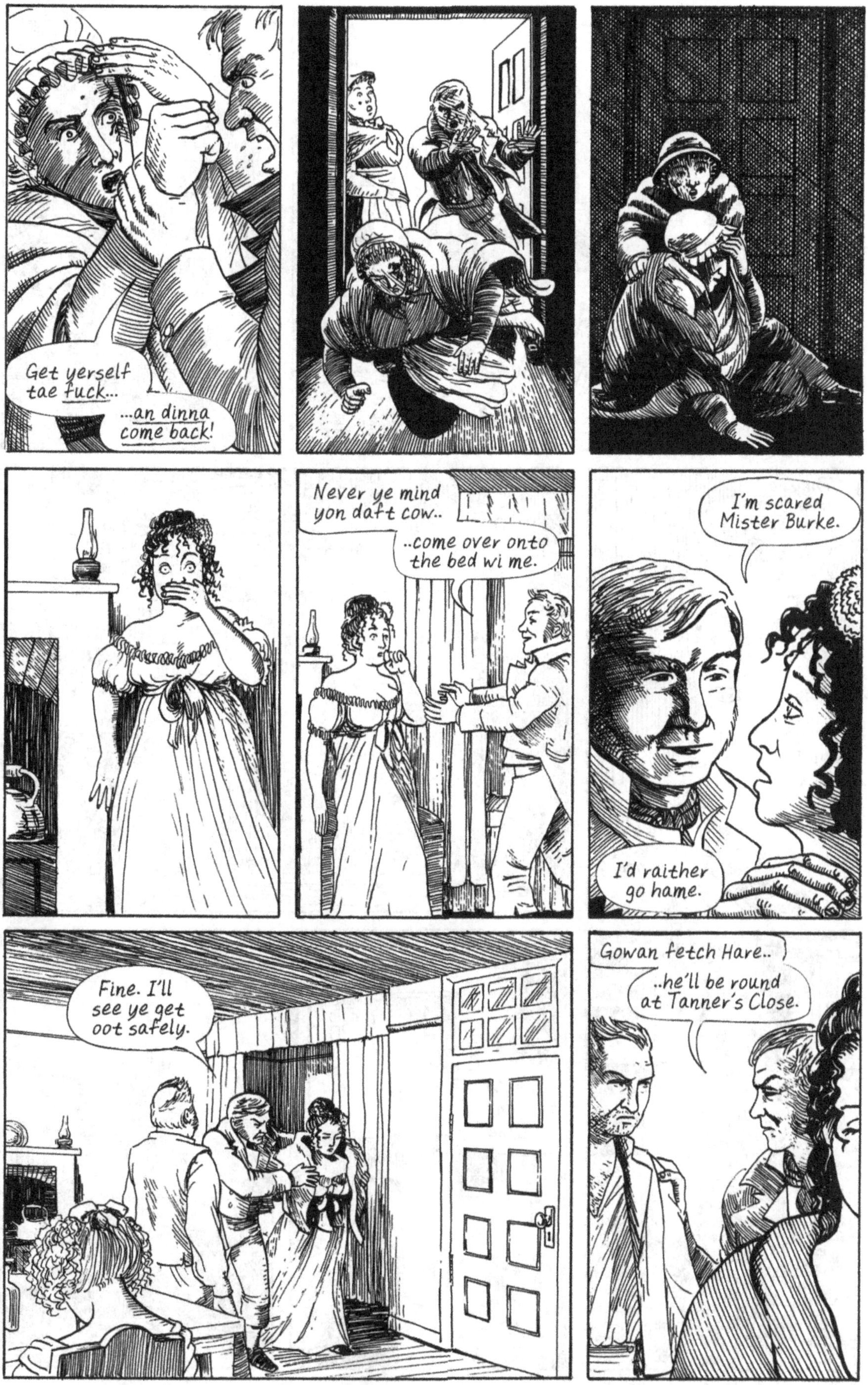
Get yerself tae fuck...
...an dinna come back!
Never ye mind yon daft cow..
..come over onto the bed wi me.
I'm scared Mister Burke.
I'd raither go hame.
Fine. I'll see ye get oot safely.
Gowan fetch Hare..
..he'll be round at Tanner's Close.

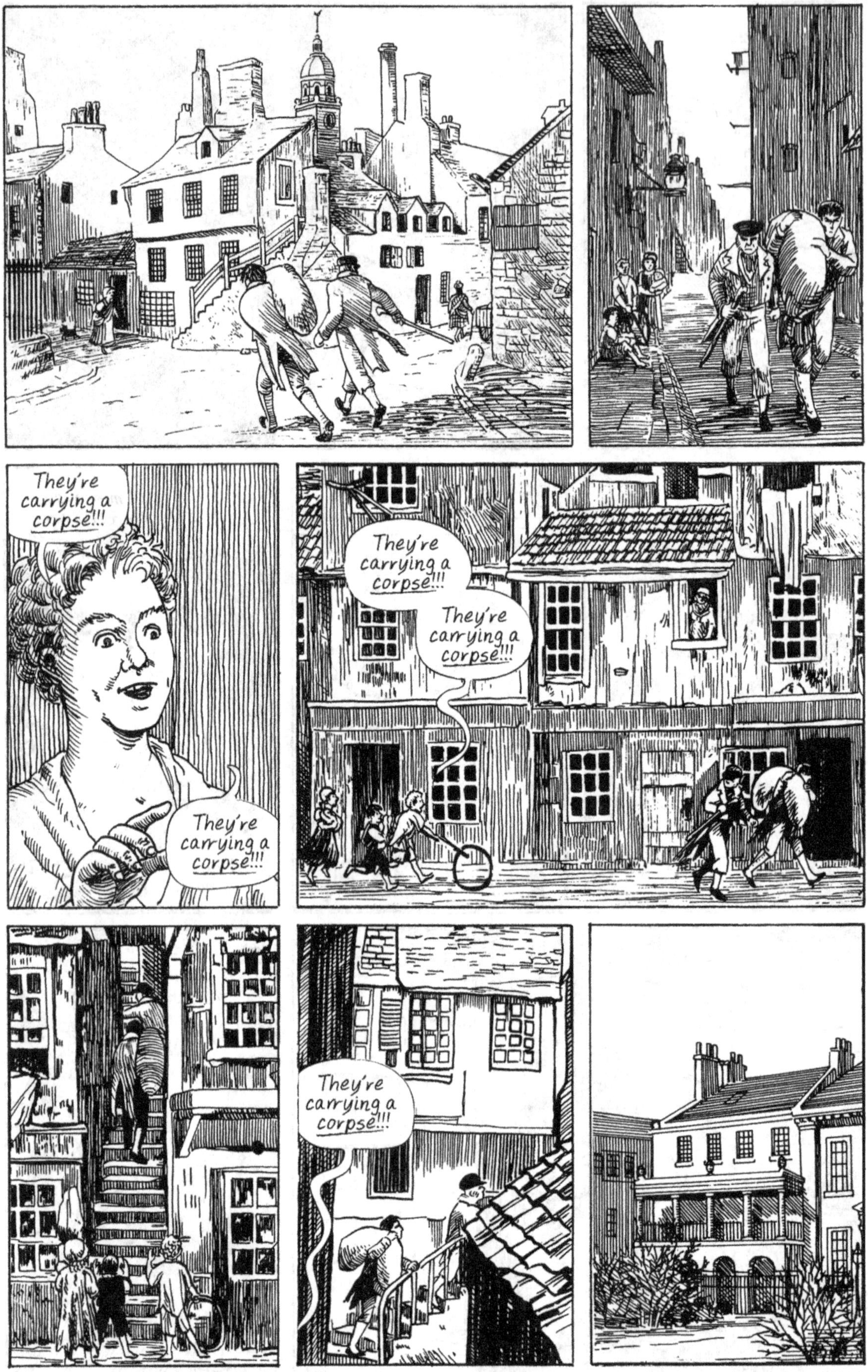
They're carrying a corpse!!!
They're carrying a corpse!!!
They're carrying a corpse!!!
They're carrying a corpse!!!
They're carrying a corpse!!!

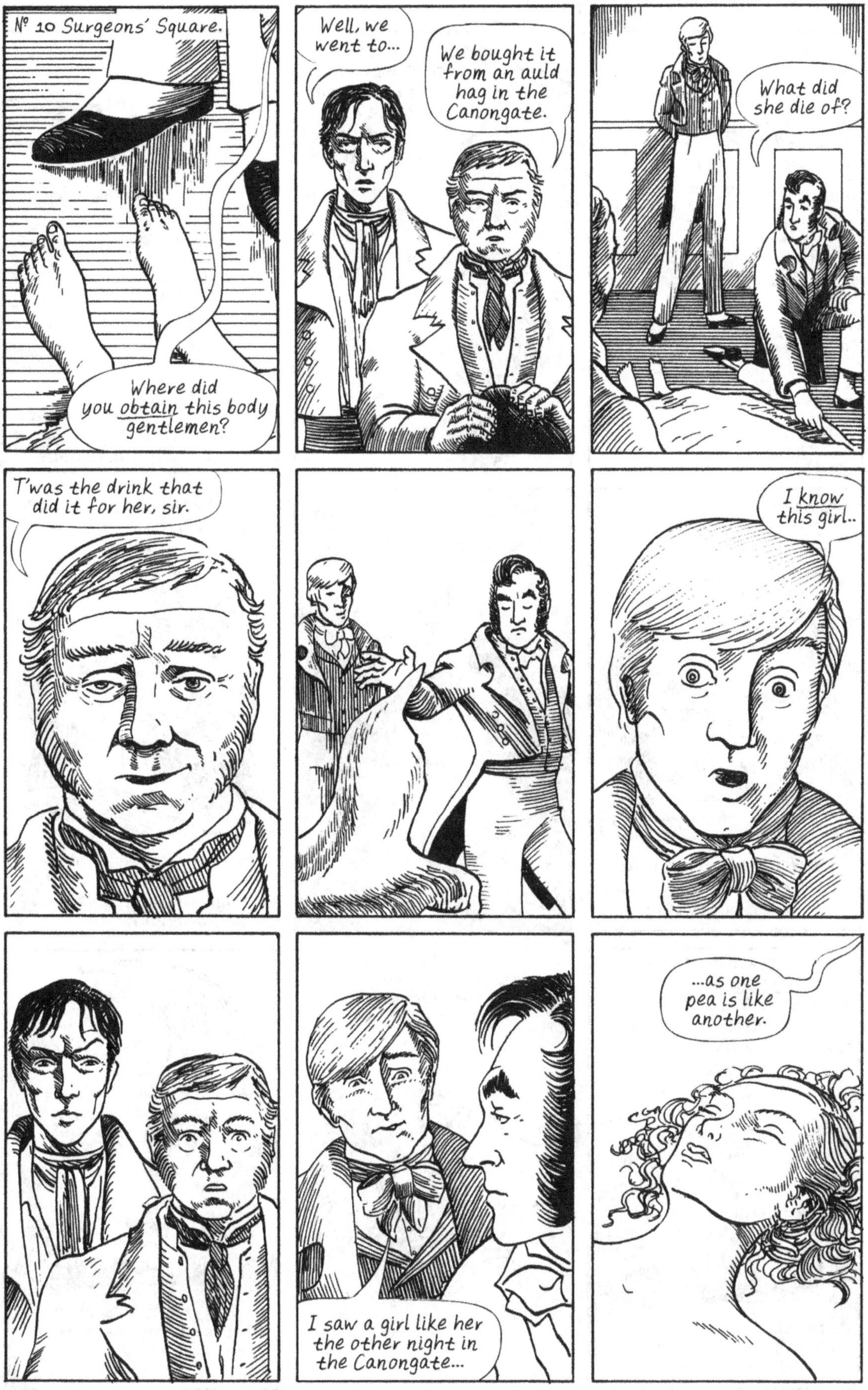
Nº 10 Surgeons' Square.
Where did you obtain this body gentlemen?
Well, we went to...
We bought it from an auld hag in the Canongate.
What did she die of?
T'was the drink that did it for her, sir.
I know this girl..
I saw a girl like her the other night in the Canongate...
...as one pea is like another.

Chapter Eight: In Cold Blood

Calton Gaol, Edinburgh. Saturday, 3 January, 1829.

The <u>Paterson</u> girl was disposed of five or six hours after she was killed...

...The body was cold, but not very stiff...

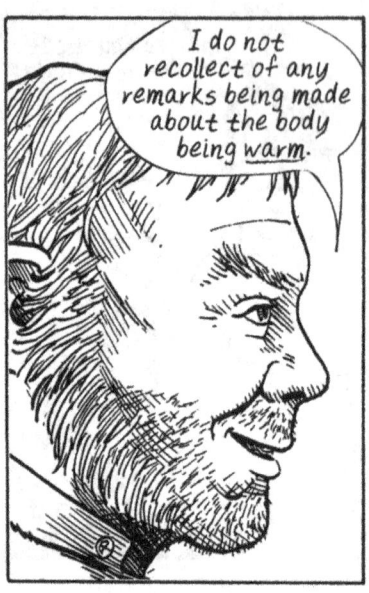

I do not recollect of any remarks being made about the body being <u>warm</u>.

And did you meet with <u>Doctor Knox</u> on this occasion?

We had no dealing with Mister Knox that time...

...but I don't think that the body would have been offered to anyone else.

"One day in September or October...

...a washer-woman had been washing in the house for some time... me and Hare suffocated her."

Soon afterwards, a woman named <u>McDougal</u>, who was a relation of Nelly's first husband, came to Broggan's house to see Nelly.

After she had been coming and going for a few days, she got drunk.

"...and was served in the same way by myself and Hare."

'Daft Jamie' was then disposed of in the manner mentioned before, except Hare was concerned in it...

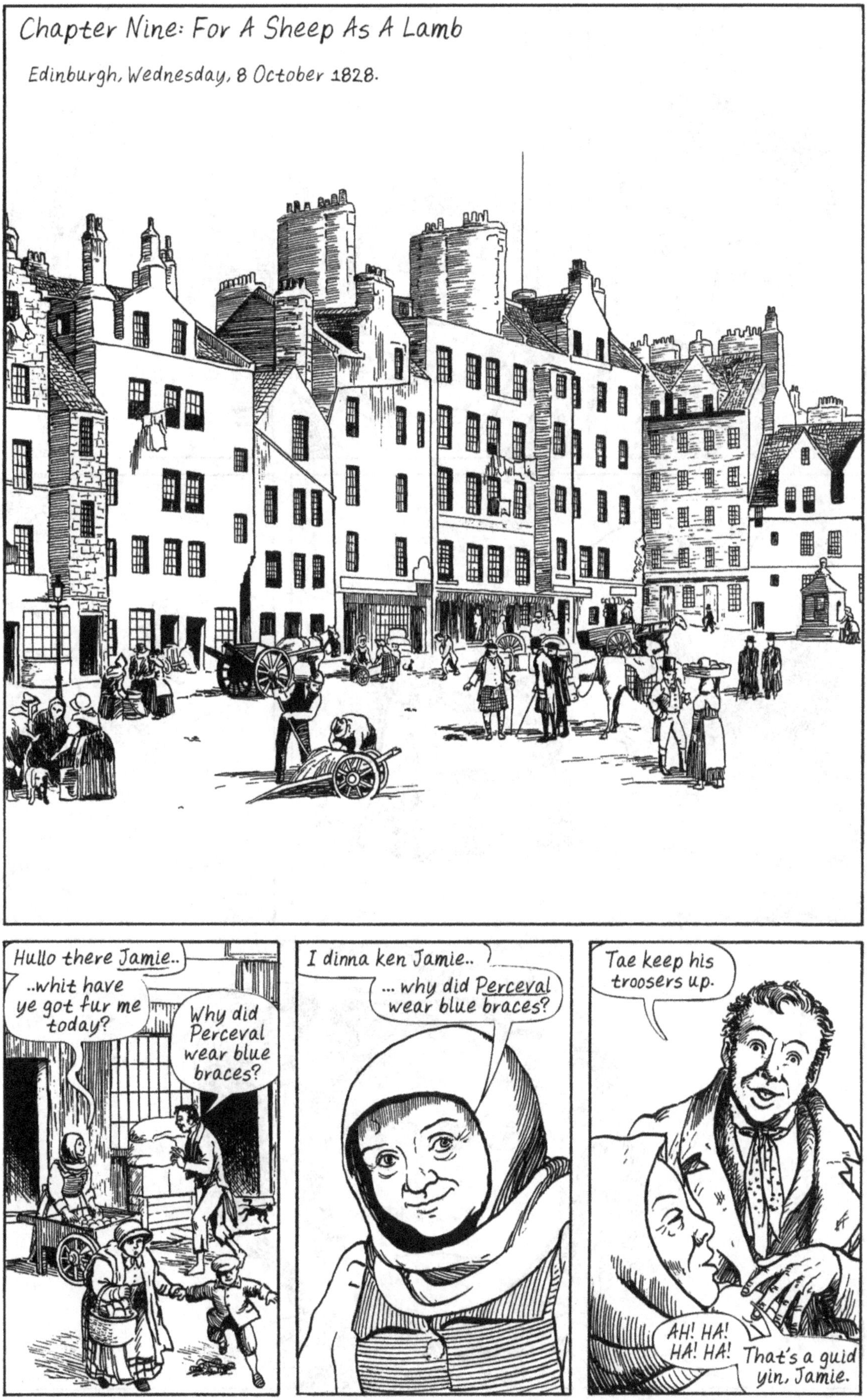
Chapter Nine: For A Sheep As A Lamb
Edinburgh, Wednesday, 8 October 1828.
Hullo there Jamie..
..whit have ye got fur me today?
Why did Perceval wear blue braces?
I dinna ken Jamie..
... why did Perceval wear blue braces?
Tae keep his troosers up.
AH! HA! HA! HA!
That's a guid yin, Jamie.

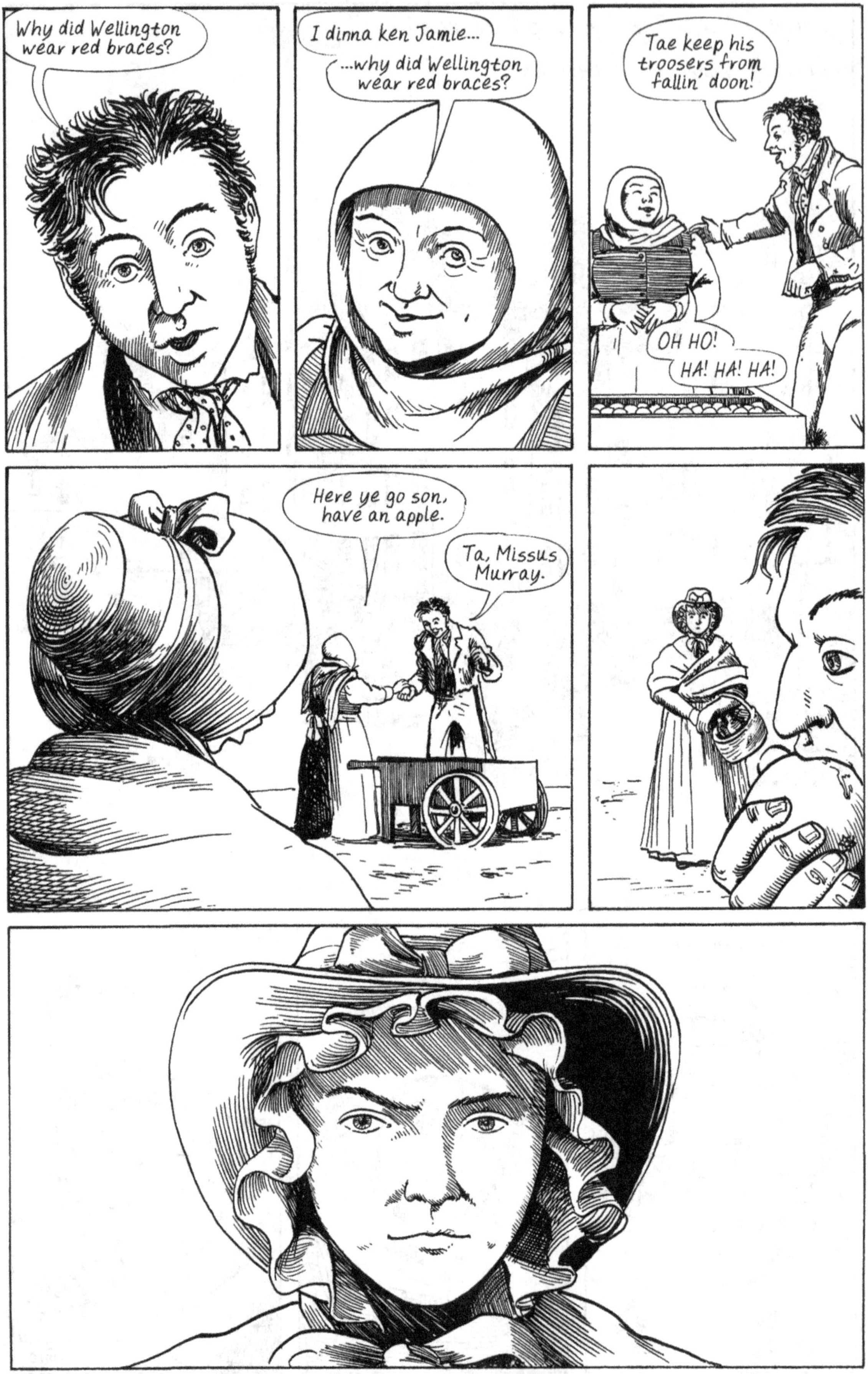
Why did Wellington wear red braces?
I dinna ken Jamie...
...why did Wellington wear red braces?
Tae keep his troosers from fallin' doon!
OH HO!
HA! HA! HA!
Here ye go son, have an apple.
Ta, Missus Murray.

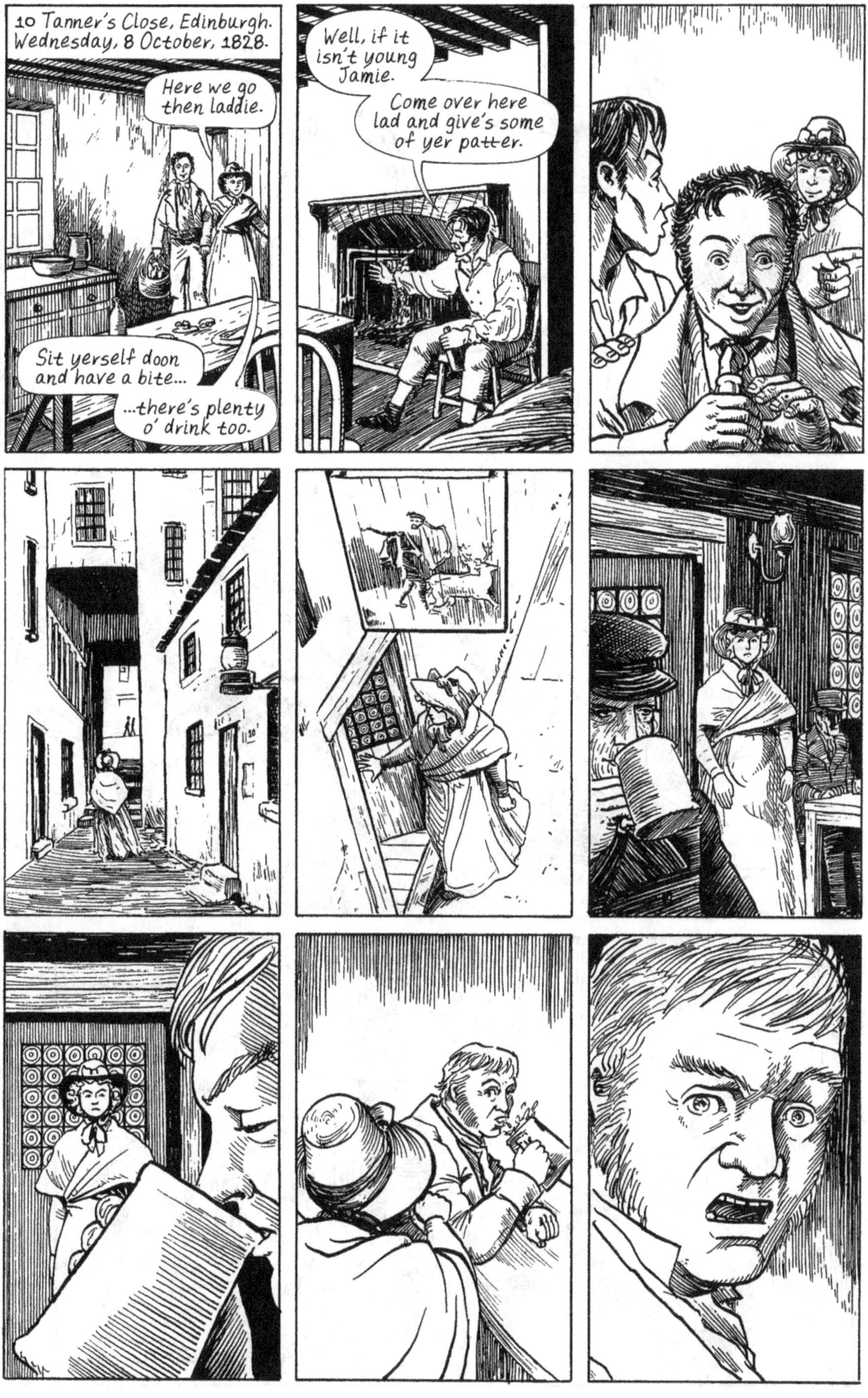

10 Tanner's Close, Edinburgh. Wednesday, 8 October, 1828.
Here we go then laddie.
Sit yerself doon and have a bite...
...there's plenty o' drink too.
Well, if it isn't young Jamie.
Come over here lad and give's some of yer patter.

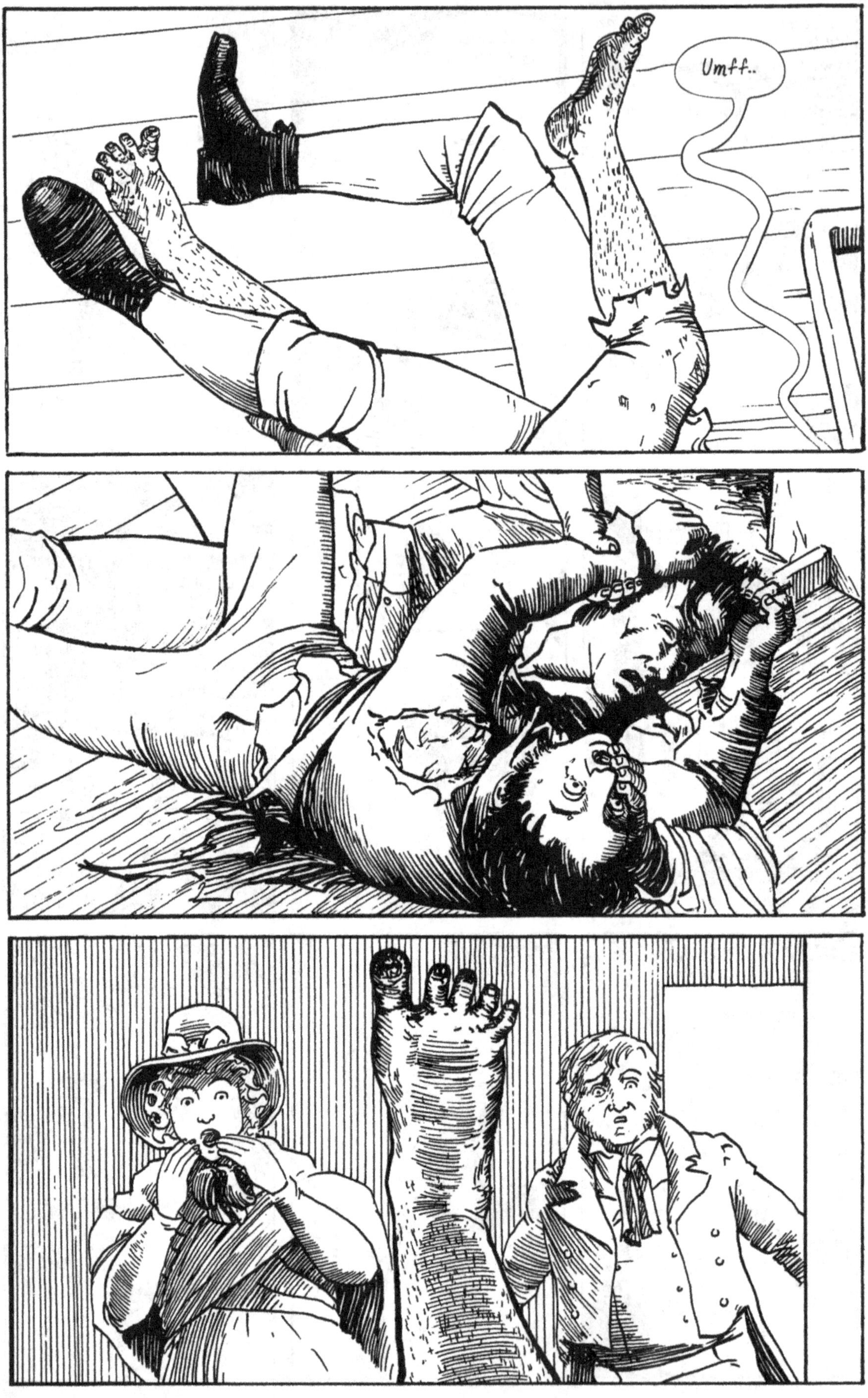
Umff..

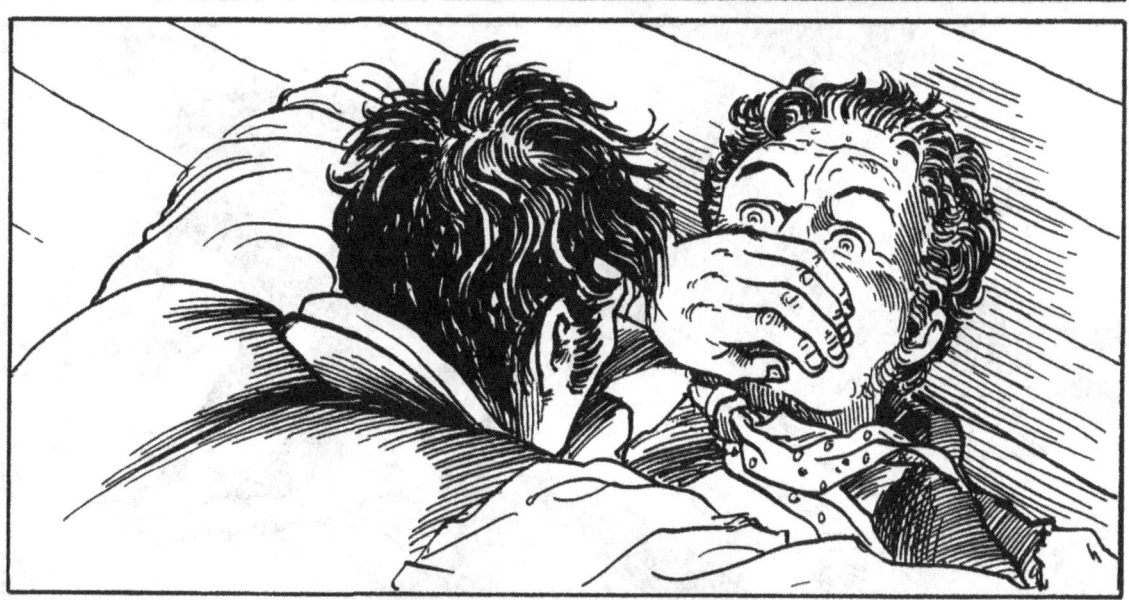

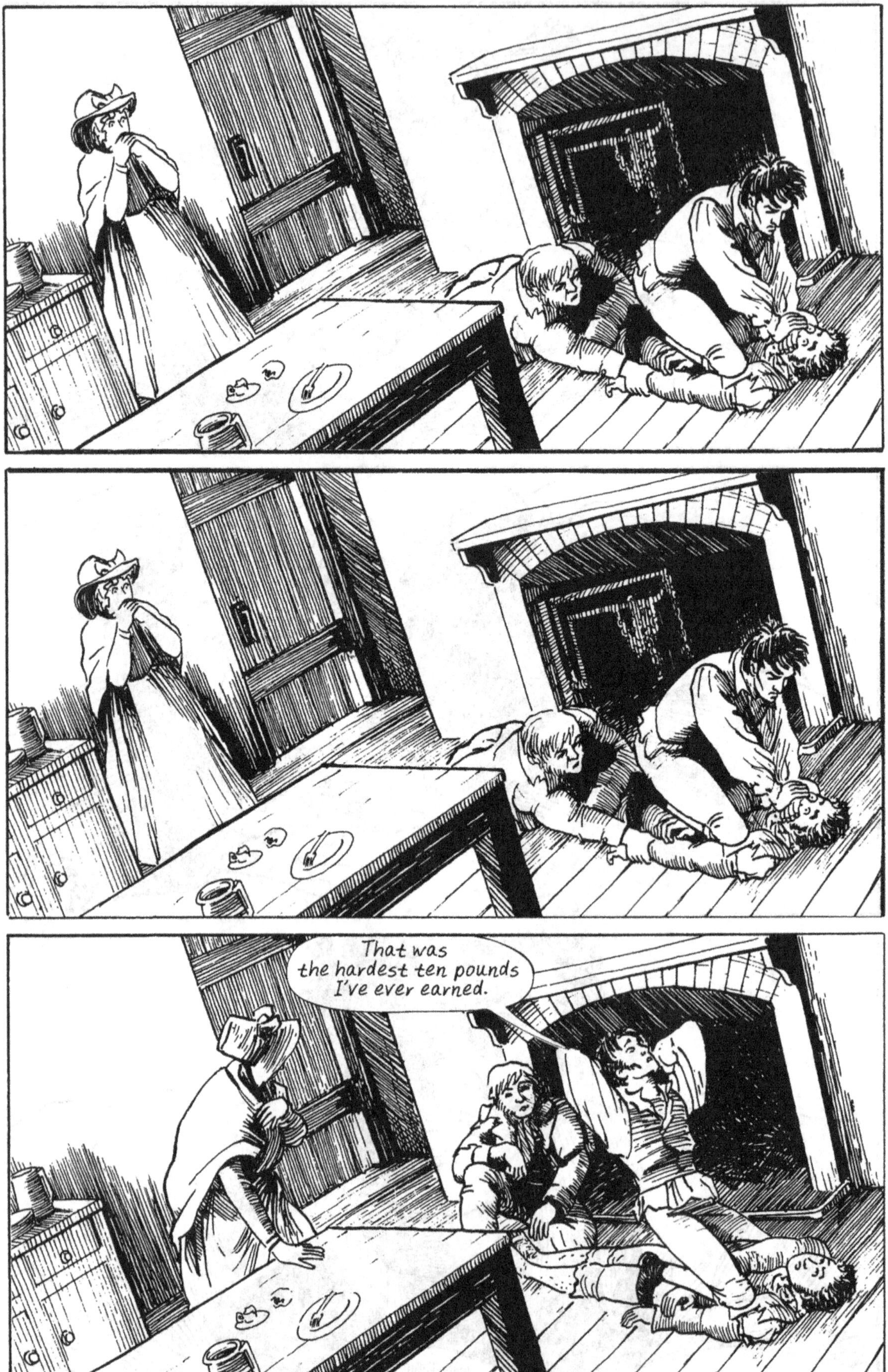
That was the hardest ten pounds I've ever earned.

Chapter Ten: The Butcher, The Thief and the Boy who bought the beef.

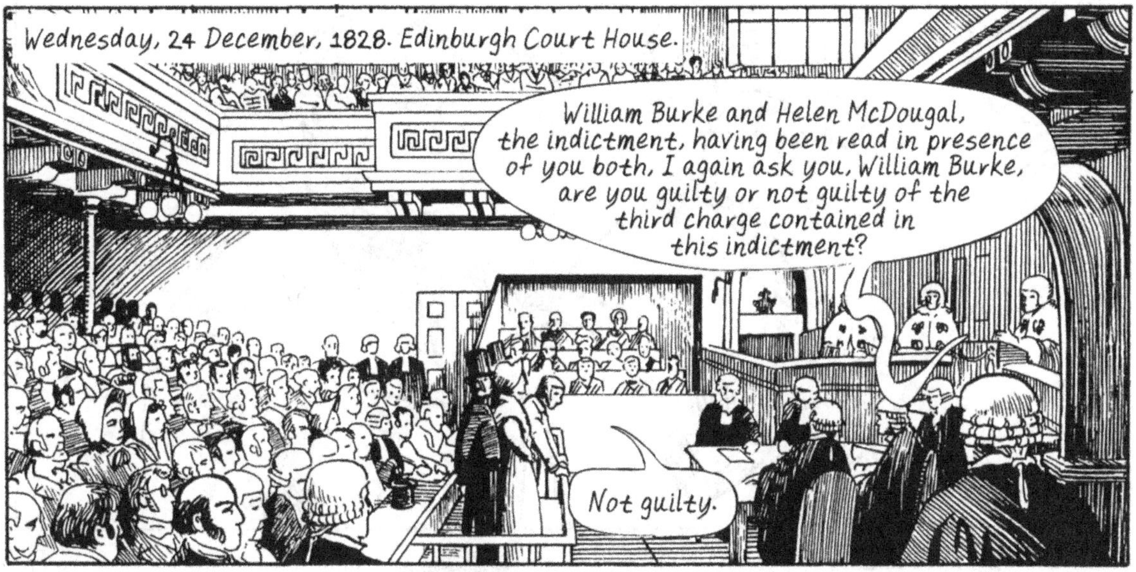
Wednesday, 24 December, 1828. Edinburgh Court House.
William Burke and Helen McDougal, the indictment, having been read in presence of you both, I again ask you, William Burke, are you guilty or not guilty of the third charge contained in this indictment?
Not guilty.

Saturday, 1 November, 1828. Broggan's Lodgings.

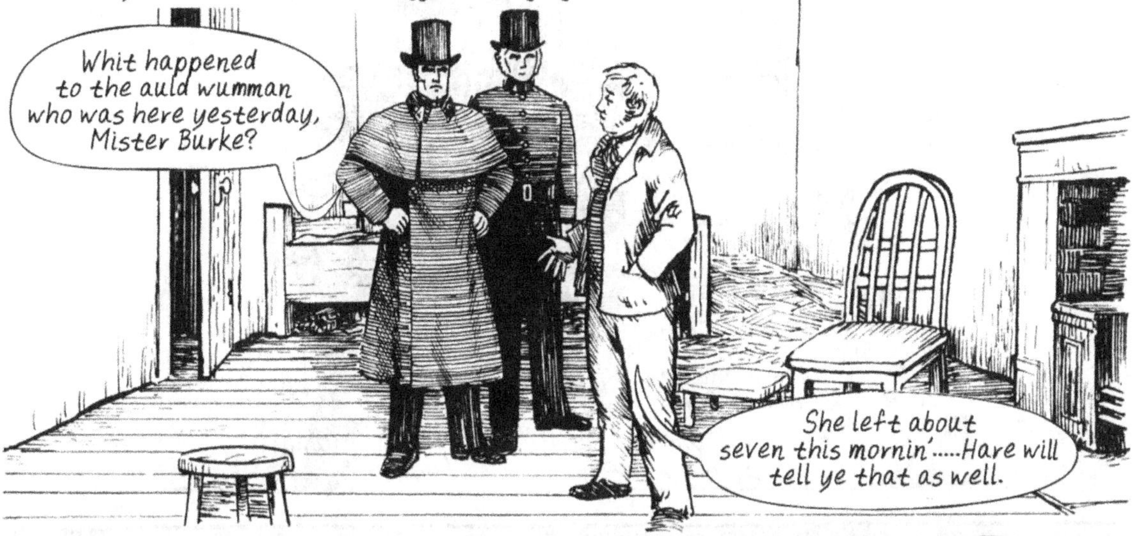
Whit happened to the auld wumman who was here yesterday, Mister Burke?
She left about seven this mornin'.....Hare will tell ye that as well.

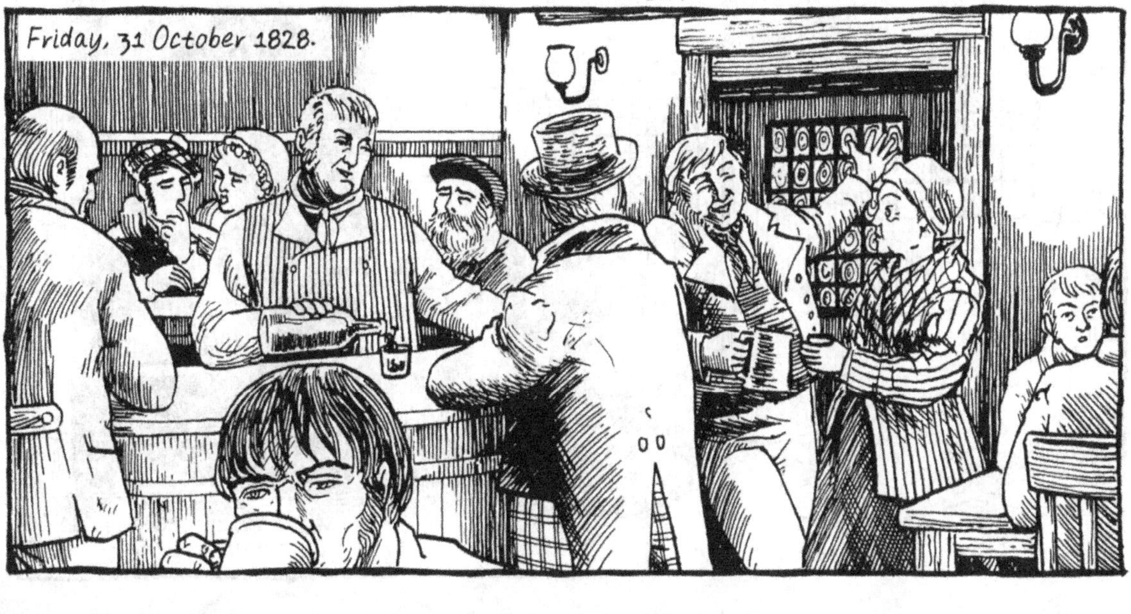
Friday, 31 October 1828.

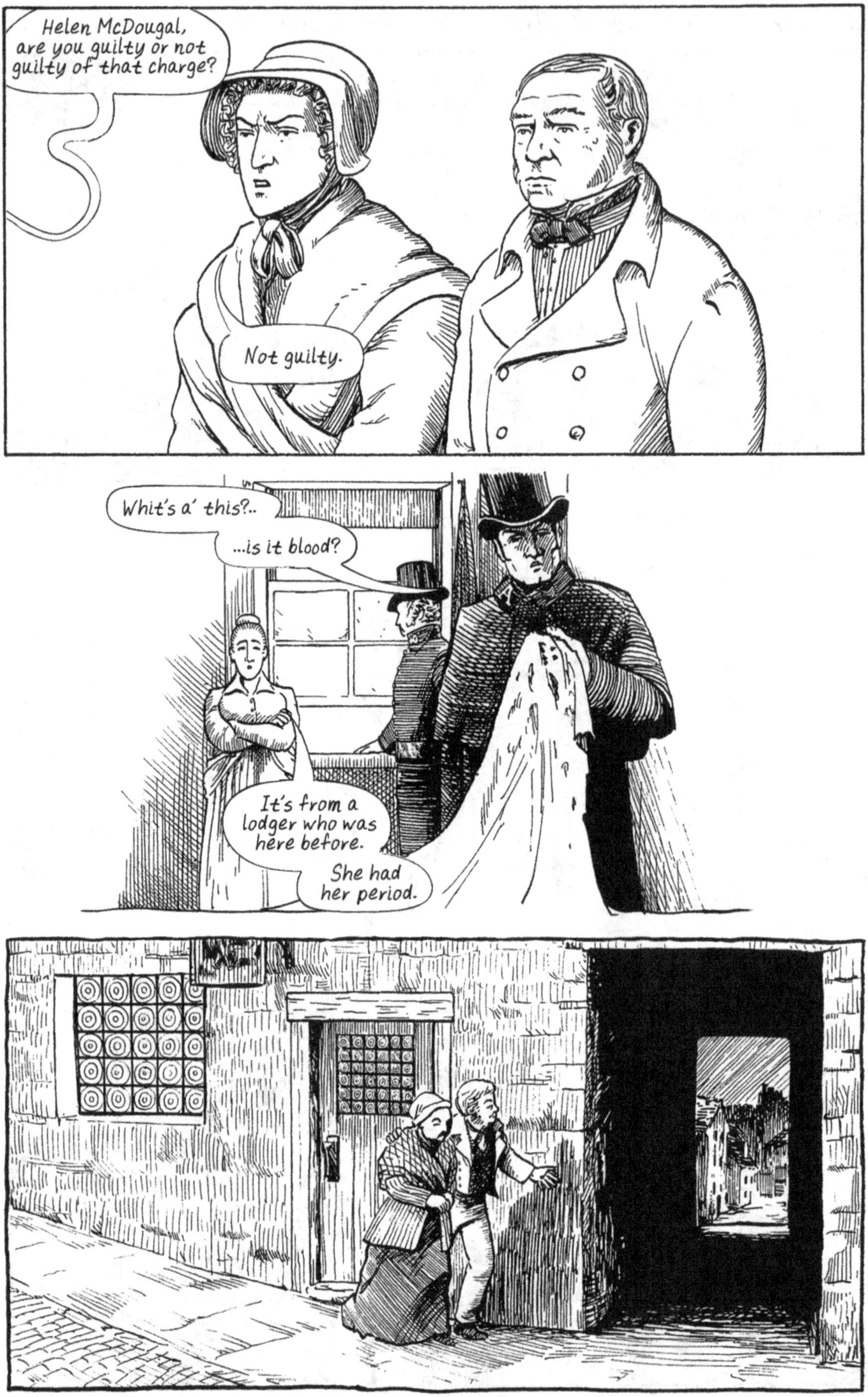
Helen McDougal, are you guilty or not guilty of that charge?
Not guilty.
Whit's a' this?..
...is it blood?
It's from a lodger who was here before.
She had her period.

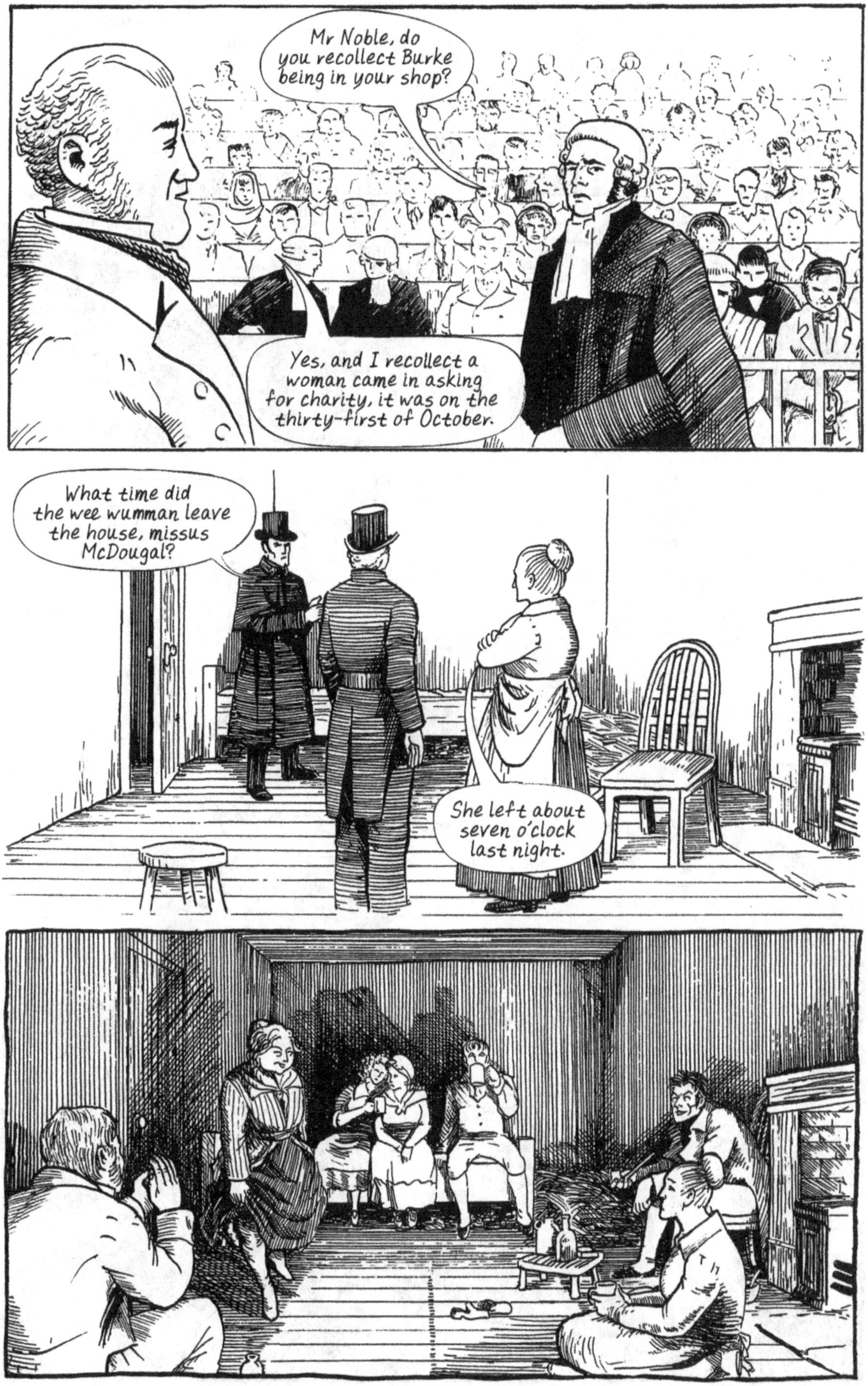
Mr Noble, do you recollect Burke being in your shop?
Yes, and I recollect a woman came in asking for charity, it was on the thirty-first of October.
What time did the wee wumman leave the house, missus McDougal?
She left about seven o'clock last night.

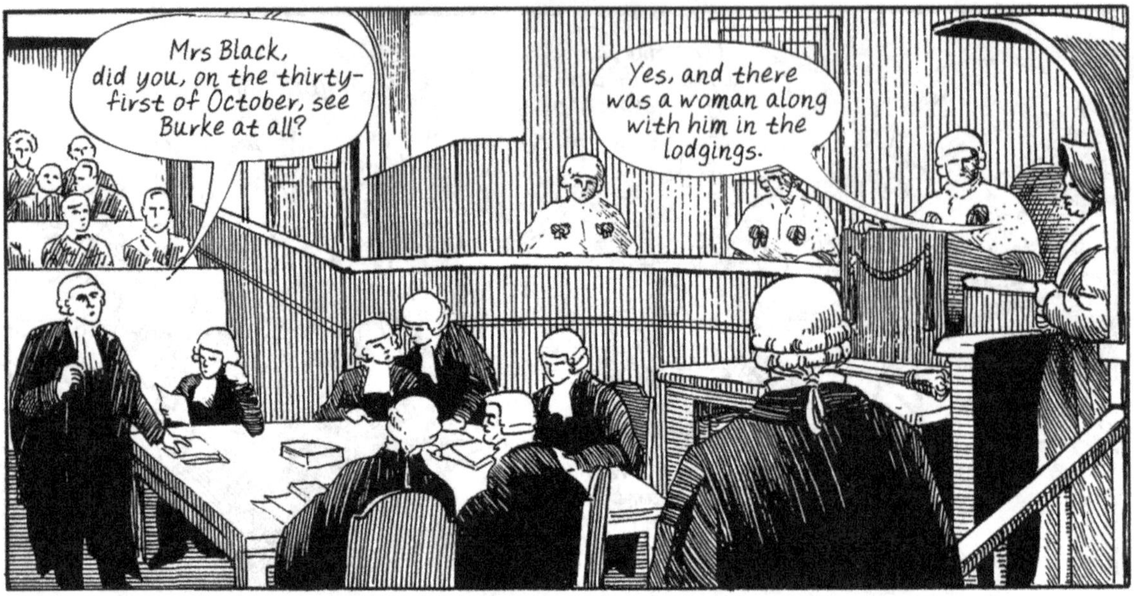
Mrs Black, did you, on the thirty-first of October, see Burke at all?
Yes, and there was a woman along with him in the lodgings.
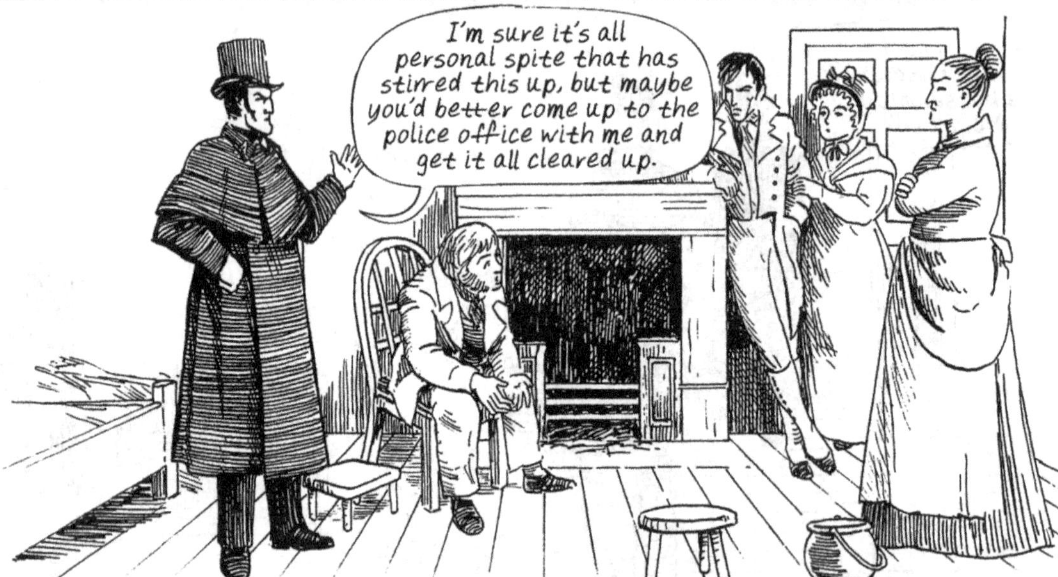
I'm sure it's all personal spite that has stirred this up, but maybe you'd better come up to the police office with me and get it all cleared up.
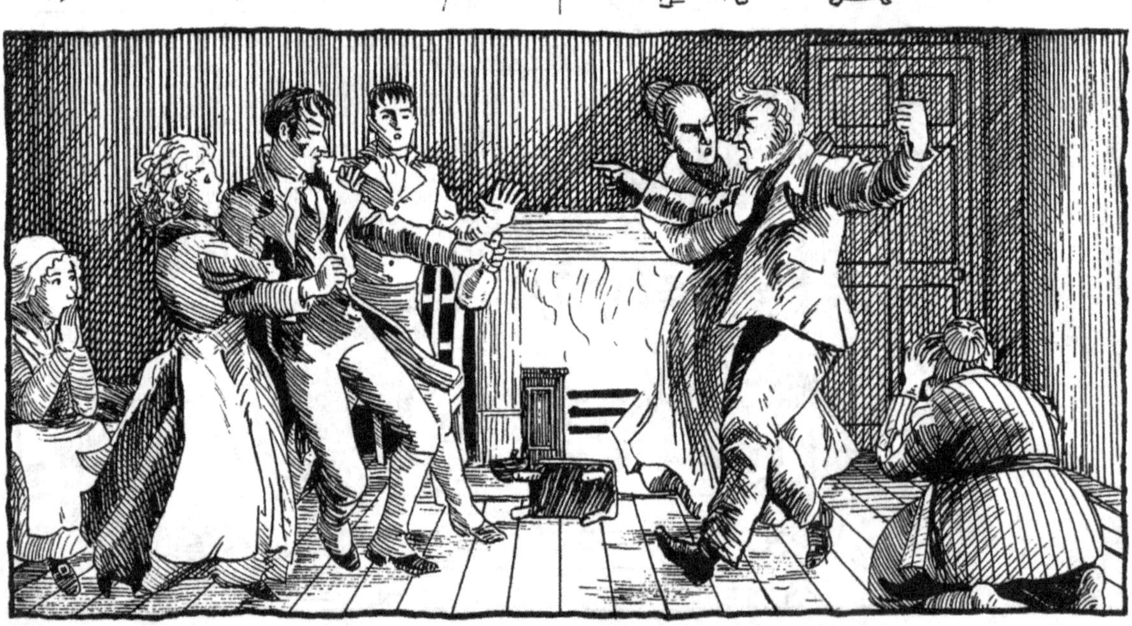

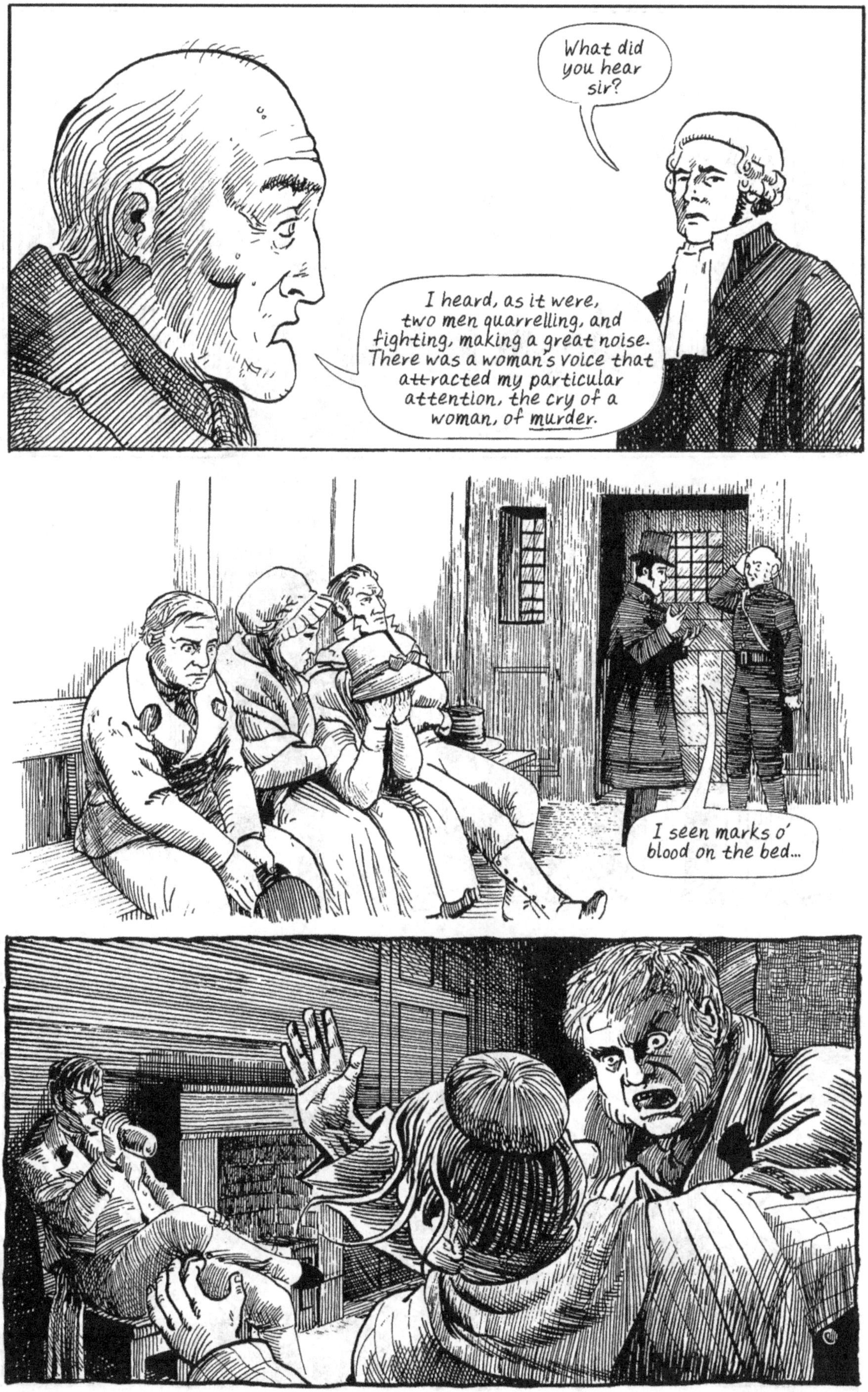
What did you hear sir?
I heard, as it were, two men quarrelling, and fighting, making a great noise. There was a woman's voice that attracted my particular attention, the cry of a woman, of murder.
I seen marks o' blood on the bed...

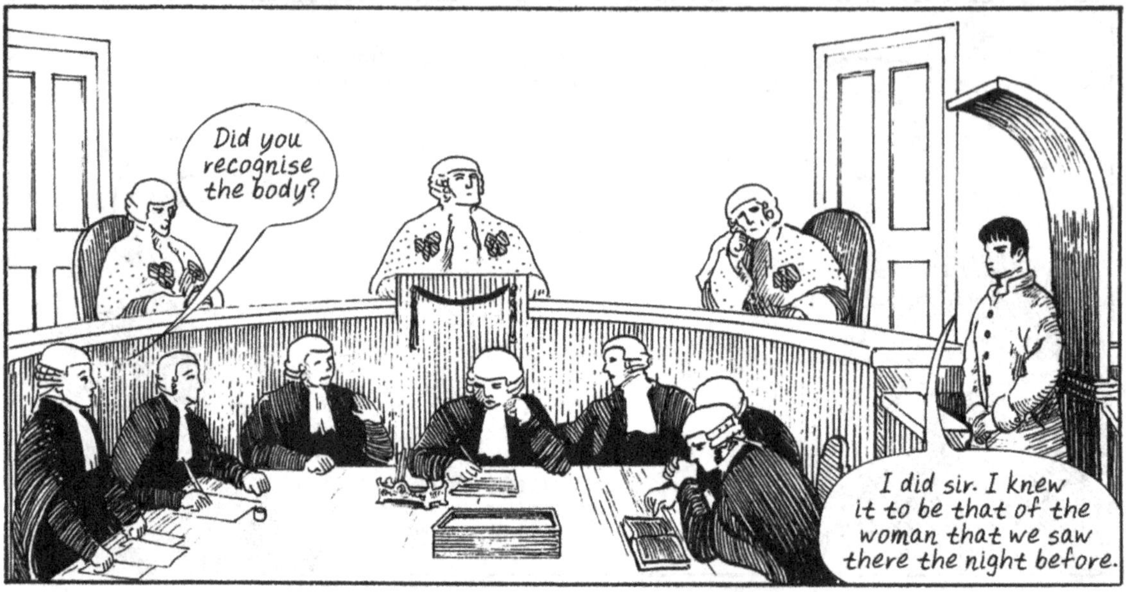
Did you recognise the body?
I did sir. I knew it to be that of the woman that we saw there the night before.

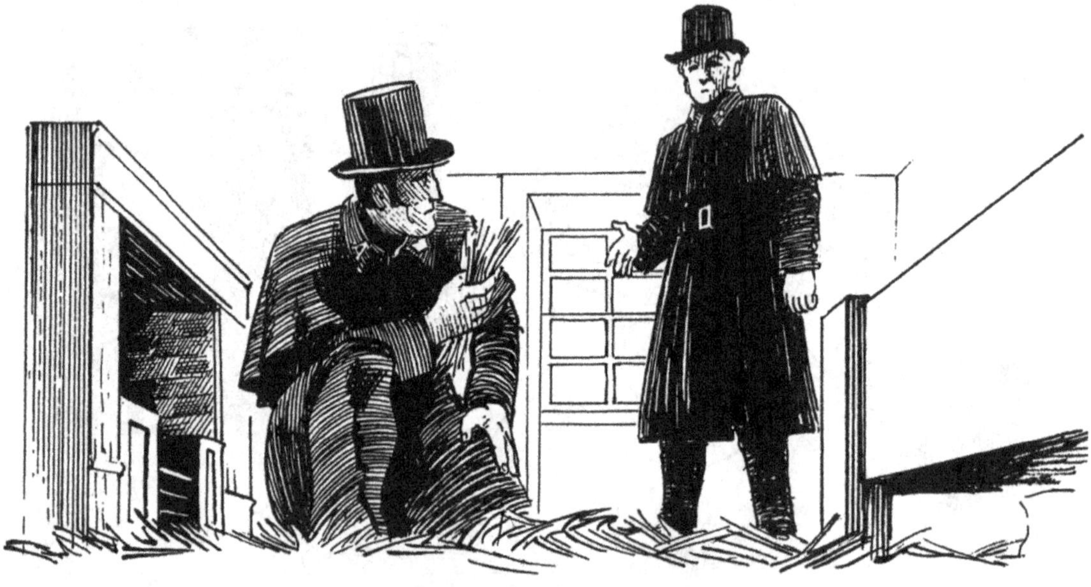

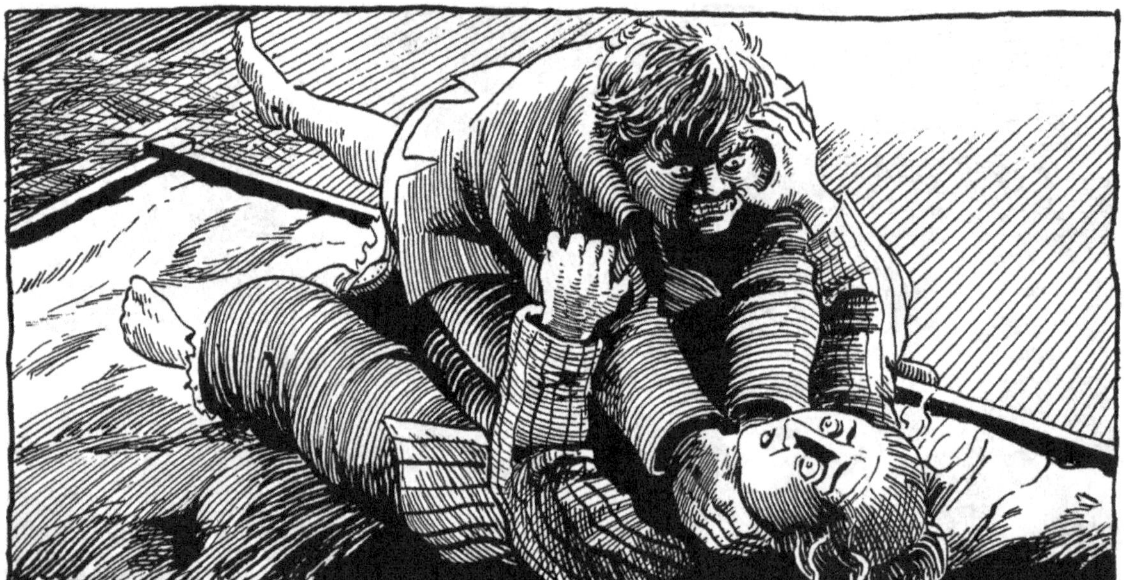

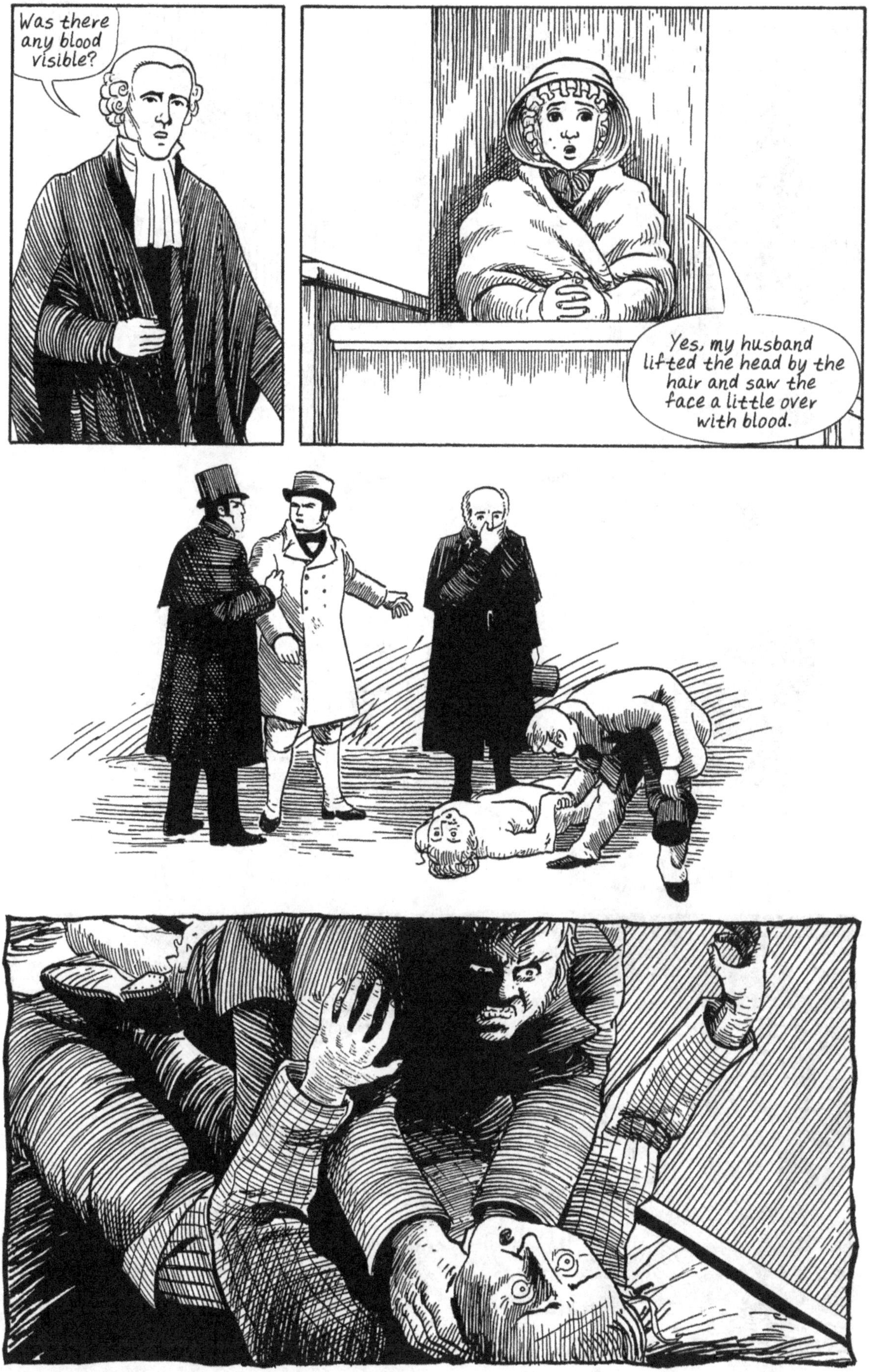
Was there any blood visible?
Yes, my husband lifted the head by the hair and saw the face a little over with blood.

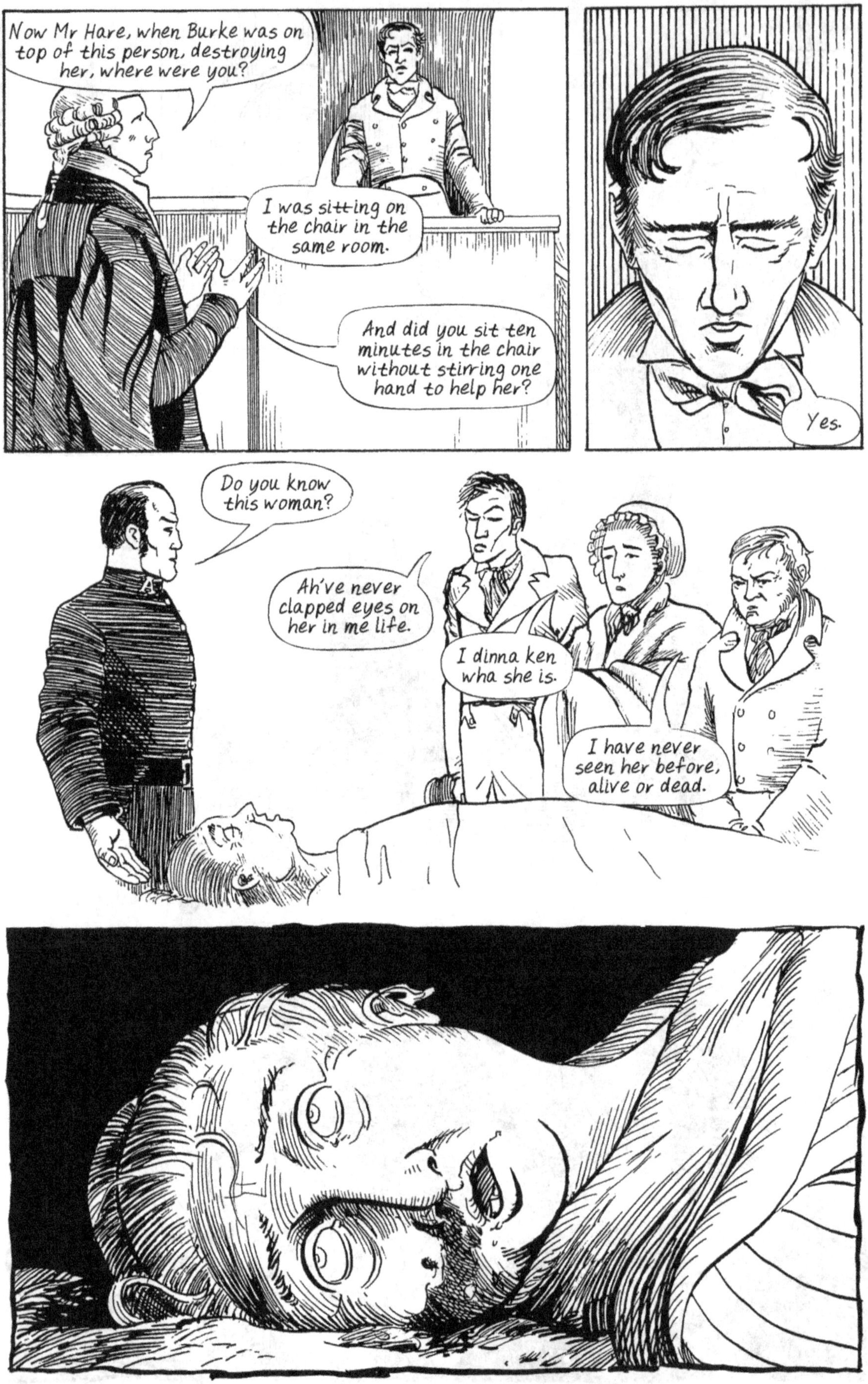
Now Mr Hare, when Burke was on top of this person, destroying her, where were you?
I was sitting on the chair in the same room.
And did you sit ten minutes in the chair without stirring one hand to help her?
Yes.
Do you know this woman?
Ah've never clapped eyes on her in me life.
I dinna ken wha she is.
I have never seen her before, alive or dead.

Chapter Eleven: To The Last

Calton Gaol, Edinburgh. Saturday, 3 January, 1829.

"The last was the old woman Docherty, for whose murder I have been convicted."

"With the exception of her, we never took any person by the throat, and we never leapt upon them."

"No suspicions were ever expressed by Dr Knox or his assistants as to where we obtained the bodies."

"And, in no way was Helen McDougal or Hare's wife ever involved in any of the murders."

"That was the whole of them — seventeen in whole."

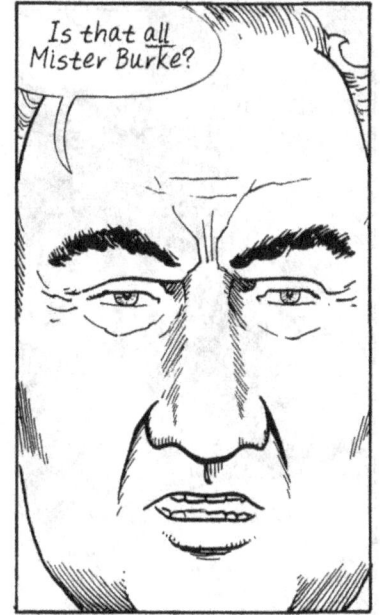

"Is that all Mister Burke?"

"That's it."

Chapter Twelve: The Sleep of The Just

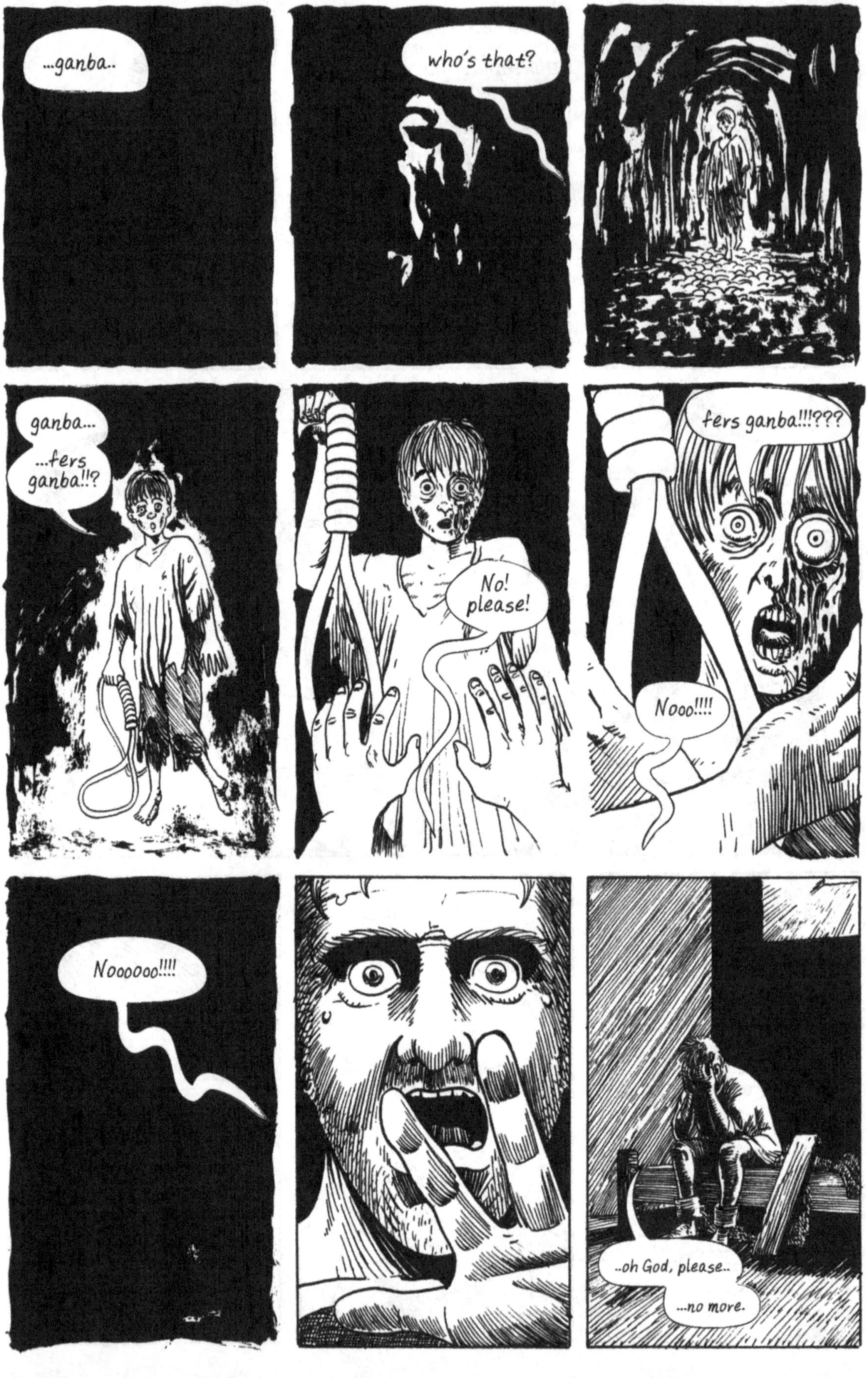
...ganba..
who's that?
ganba...
...fers ganba!!?
No! please!
fers ganba!!!???
Nooo!!!!
Noooooo!!!!
..oh God, please..
...no more.

Chapter Thirteen: The Last of Mister Burke

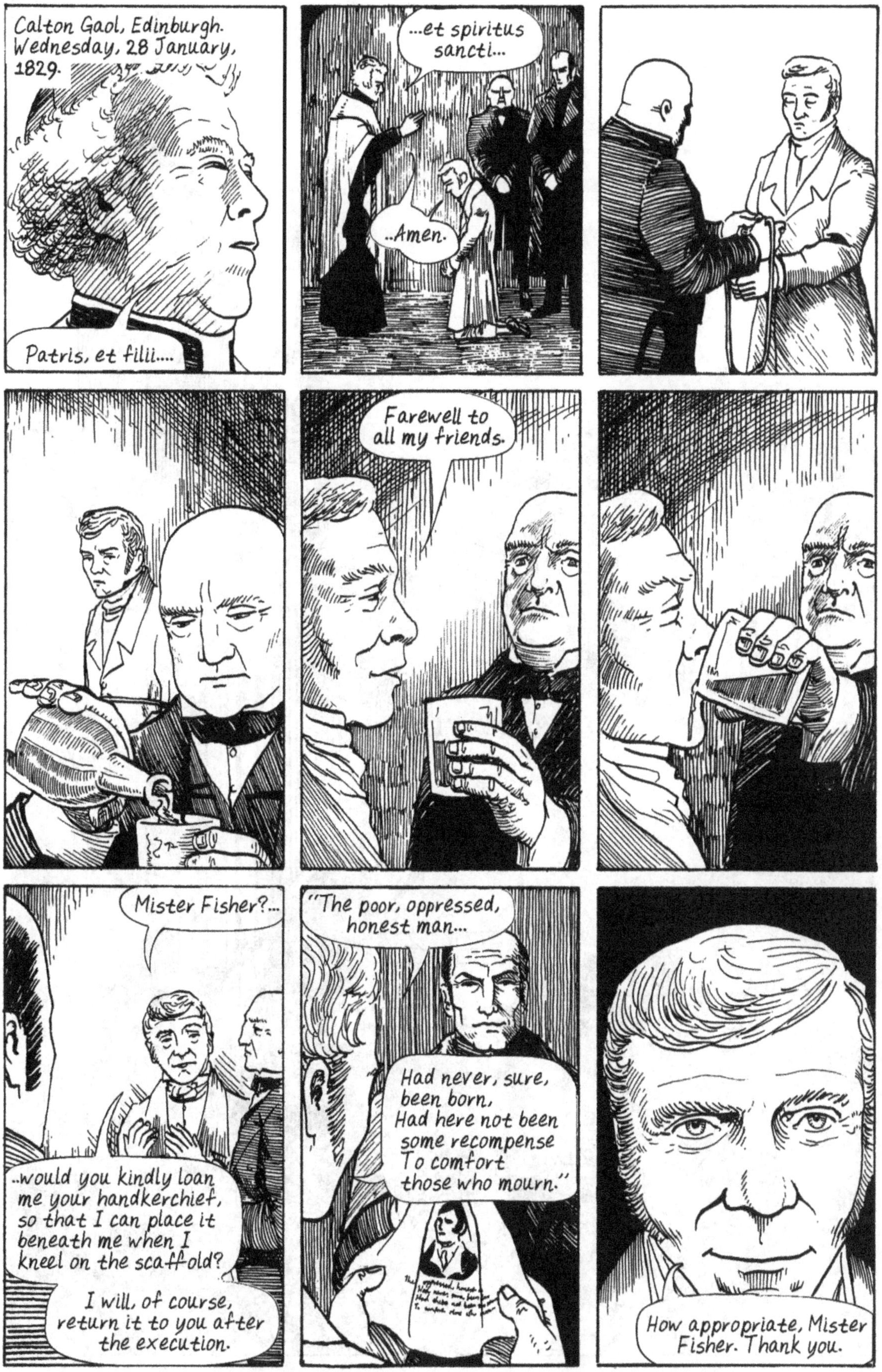
Calton Gaol, Edinburgh. Wednesday, 28 January, 1829.
Patris, et filii....
...et spiritus sancti...
..Amen.
Farewell to all my friends.
Mister Fisher?...
..would you kindly loan me your handkerchief, so that I can place it beneath me when I kneel on the scaffold?
I will, of course, return it to you after the execution.
"The poor, oppressed, honest man...
Had never, sure, been born, Had here not been some recompense To comfort those who mourn."
How appropriate, Mister Fisher. Thank you.

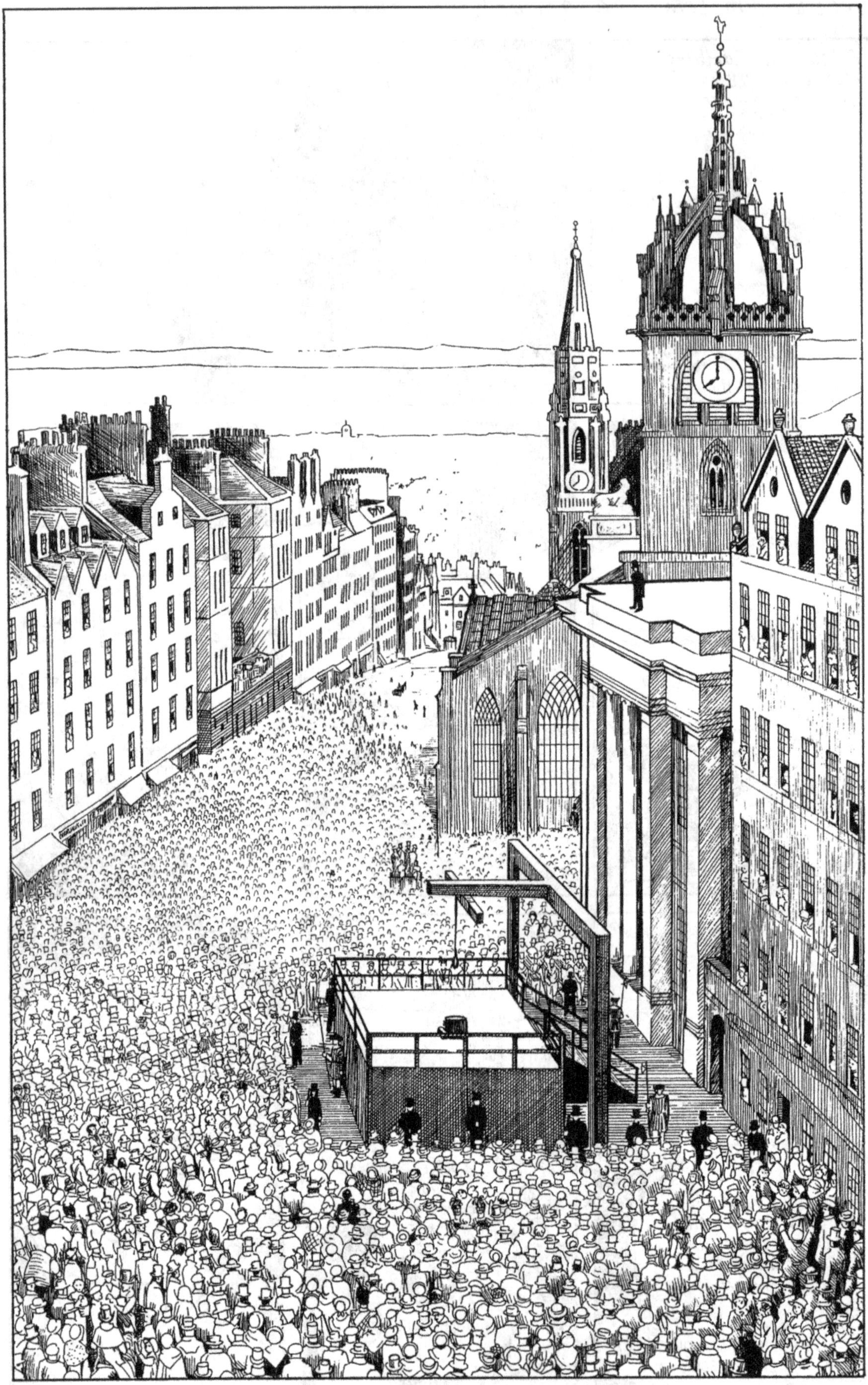

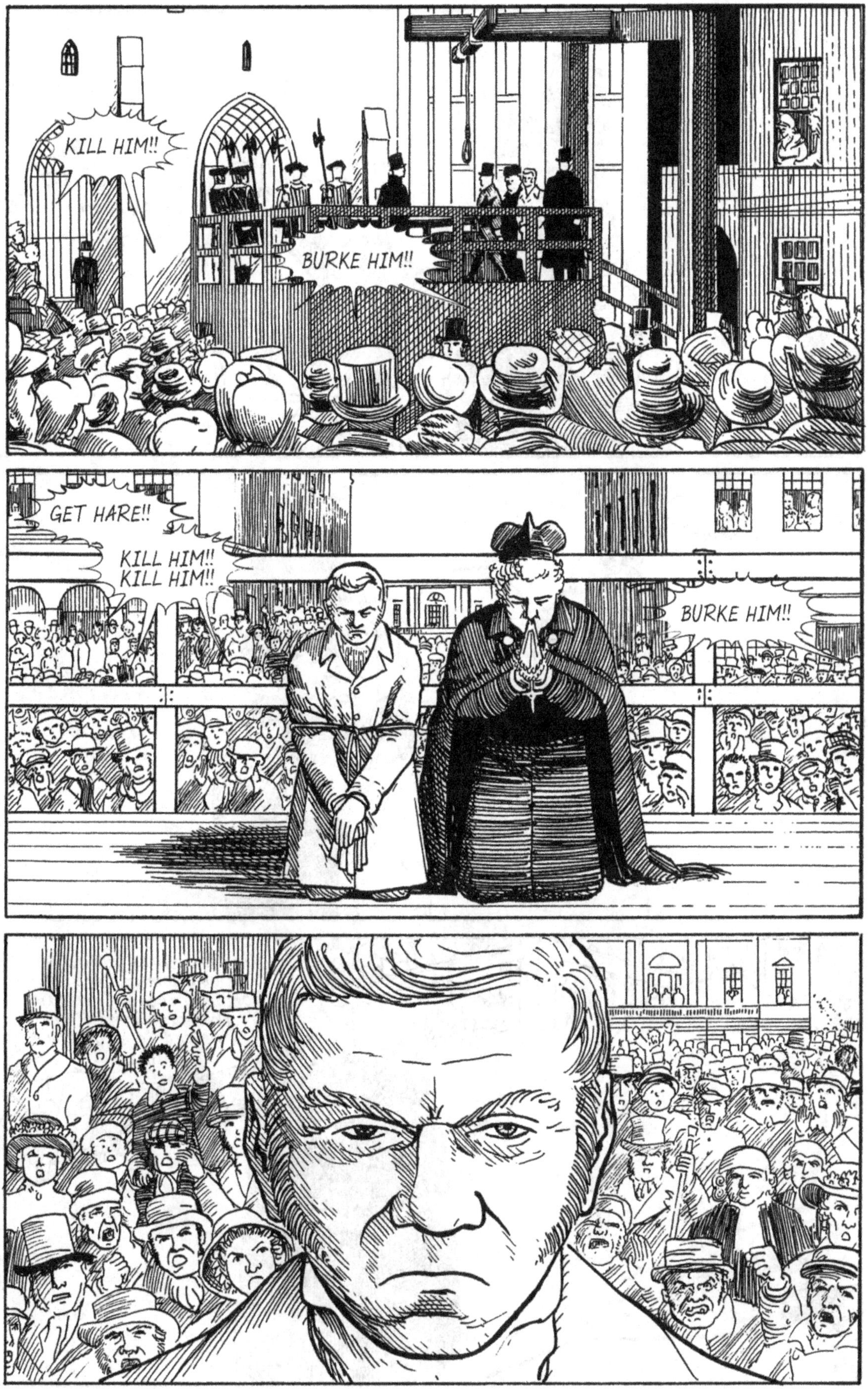
KILL HIM!!
BURKE HIM!!
GET HARE!!
KILL HIM!! KILL HIM!!
BURKE HIM!!

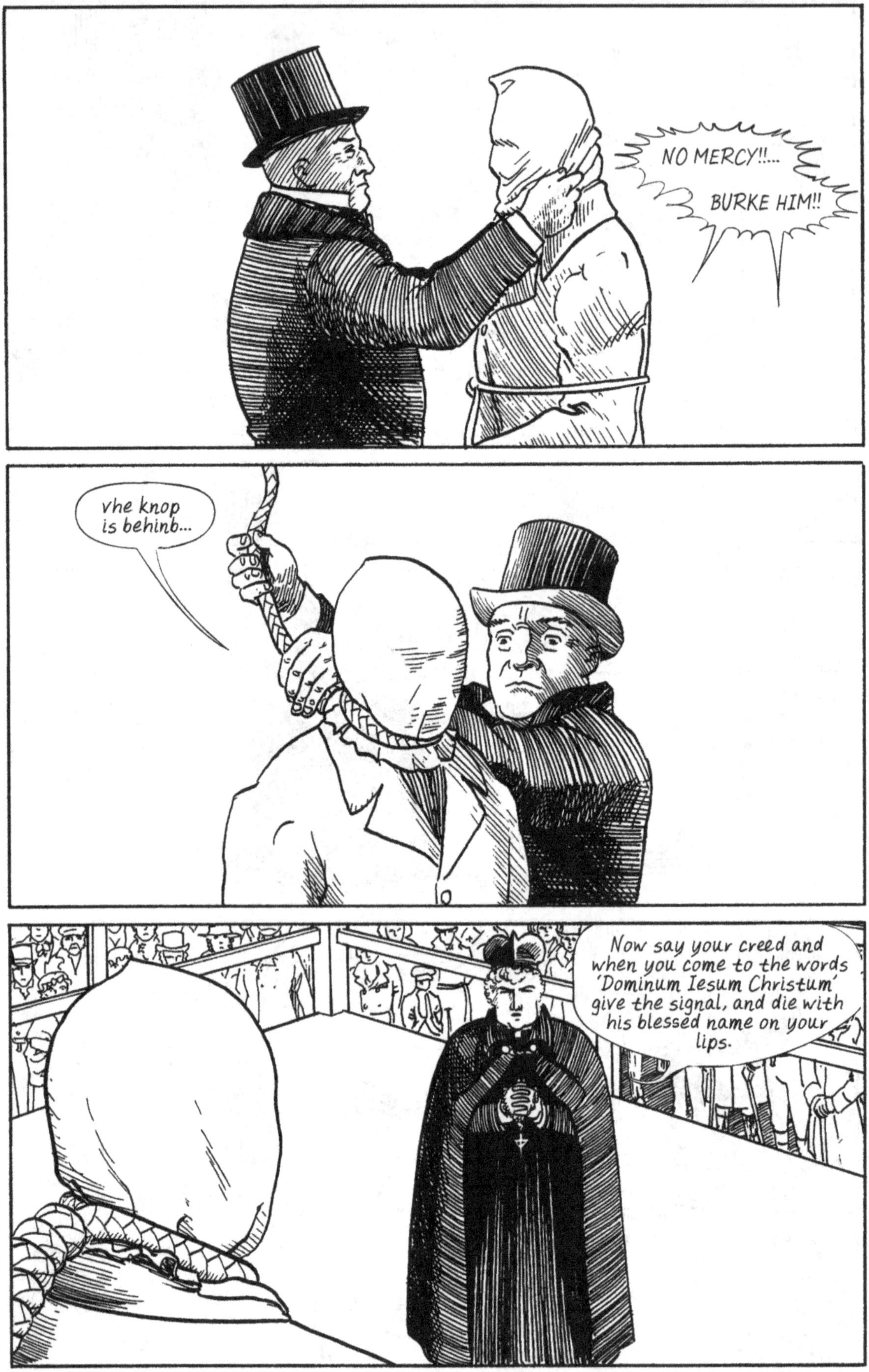
NO MERCY!!...
BURKE HIM!!
vhe knop is behinb...
Now say your creed and when you come to the words 'Dominum Iesum Christum' give the signal, and die with his blessed name on your lips.

creffo immm oomum deum..
..paffrem ommiffoffemffem...
....faffacforem caff et fferrayy..
KILL HIM!! KILL HIM!!
..viffibiffum ommium eff i.;;...mmffiffibwum..
...eft in ummum bomimum Ieffum fyystum.

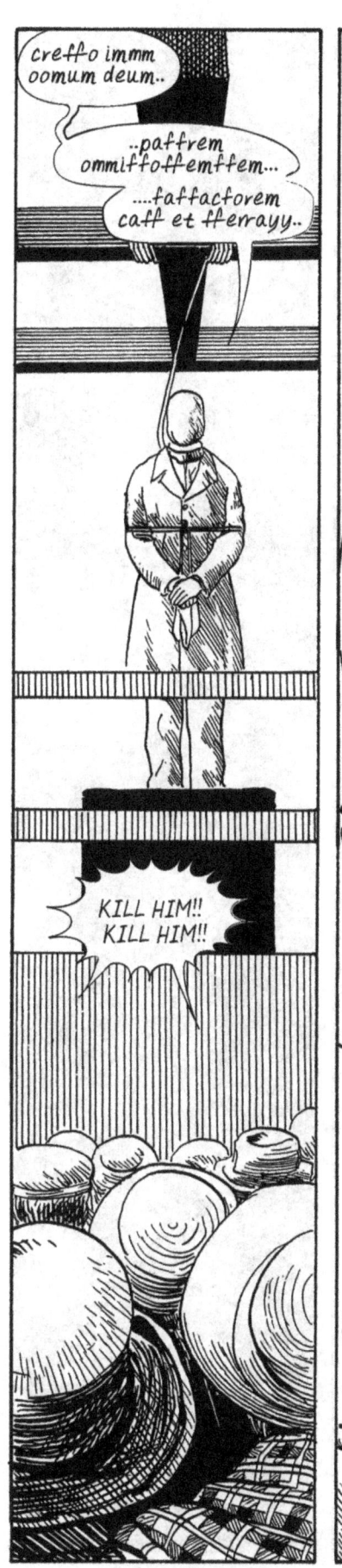

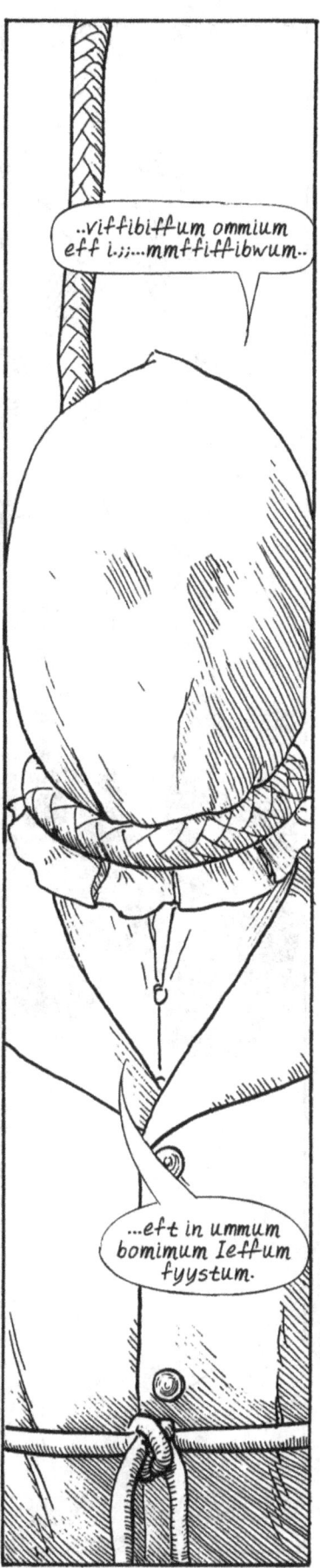

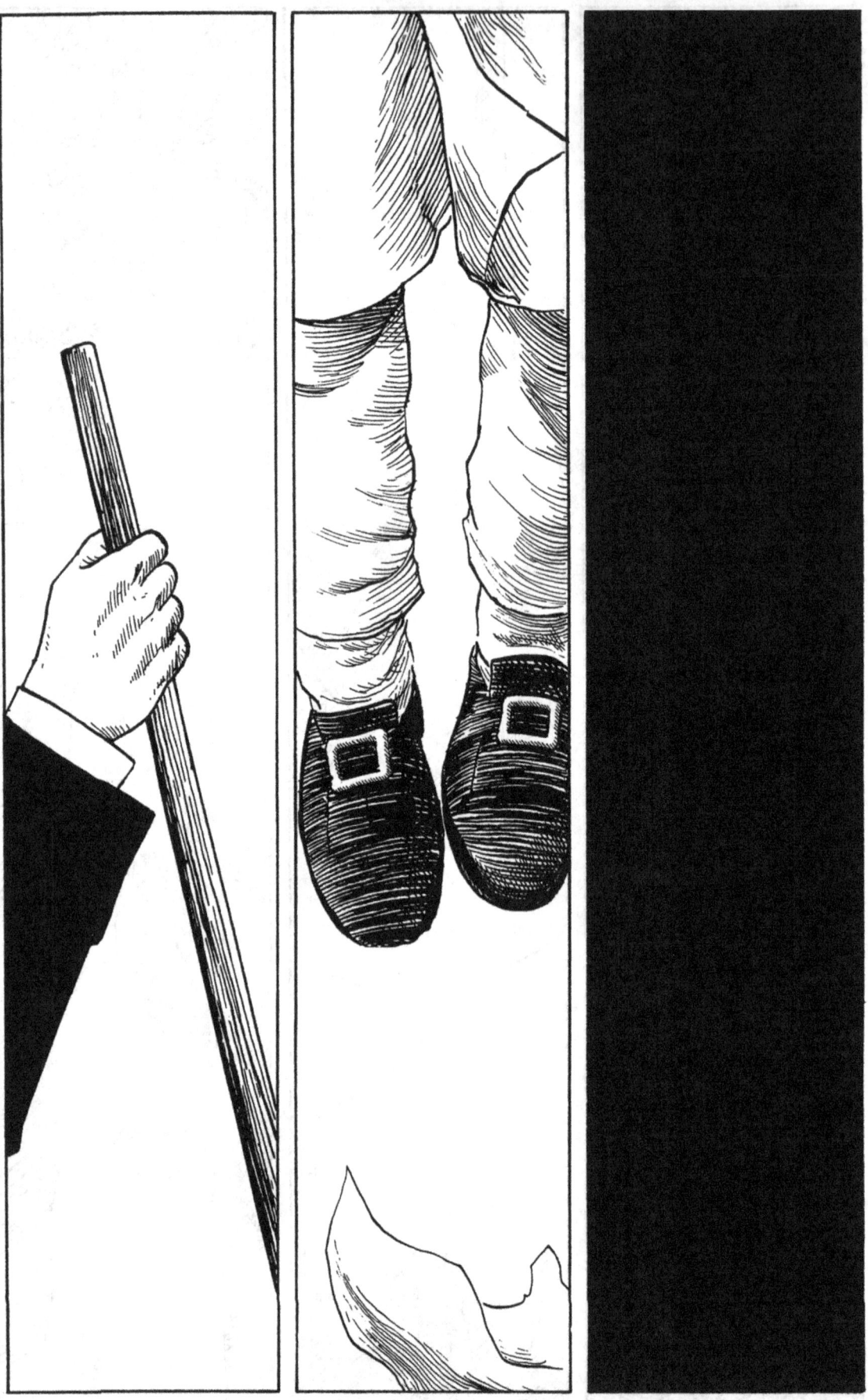

Chapter Fourteen: The Last of Mister Black

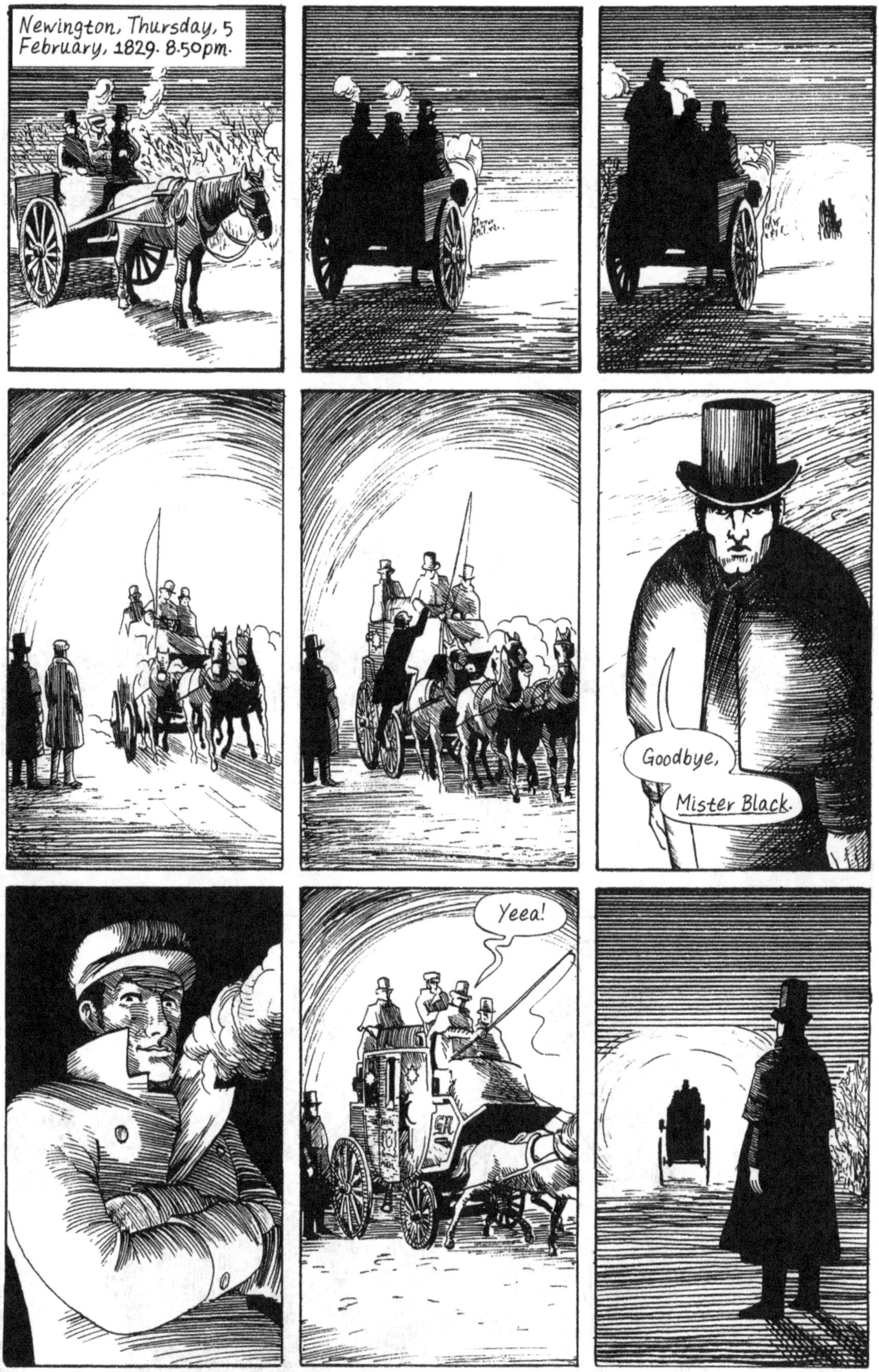

Newington, Thursday, 5 February, 1829. 8.50pm.
Goodbye, Mister Black.
Yeea!

Chapter Fifteen: The Clearing

Edinburgh. Friday, 6 February, 1829.

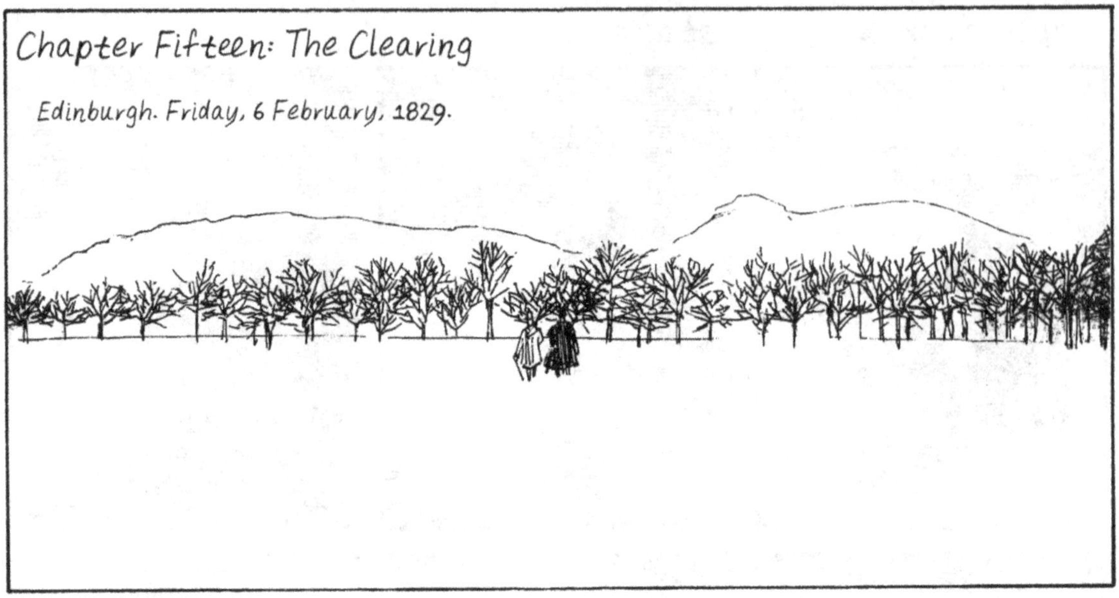

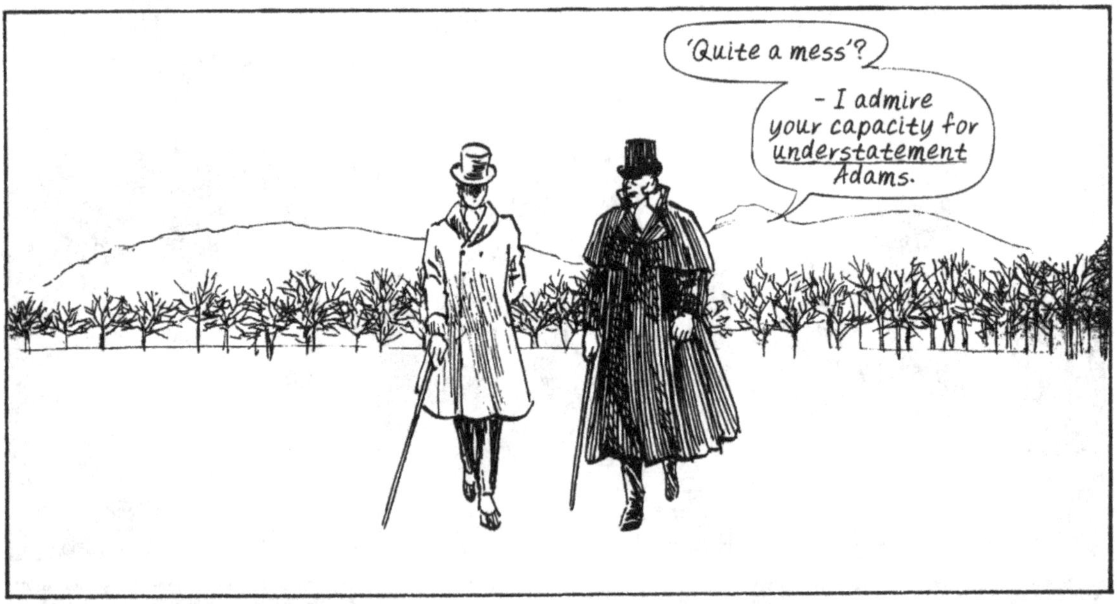

'Quite a mess'?
- I admire your capacity for understatement Adams.

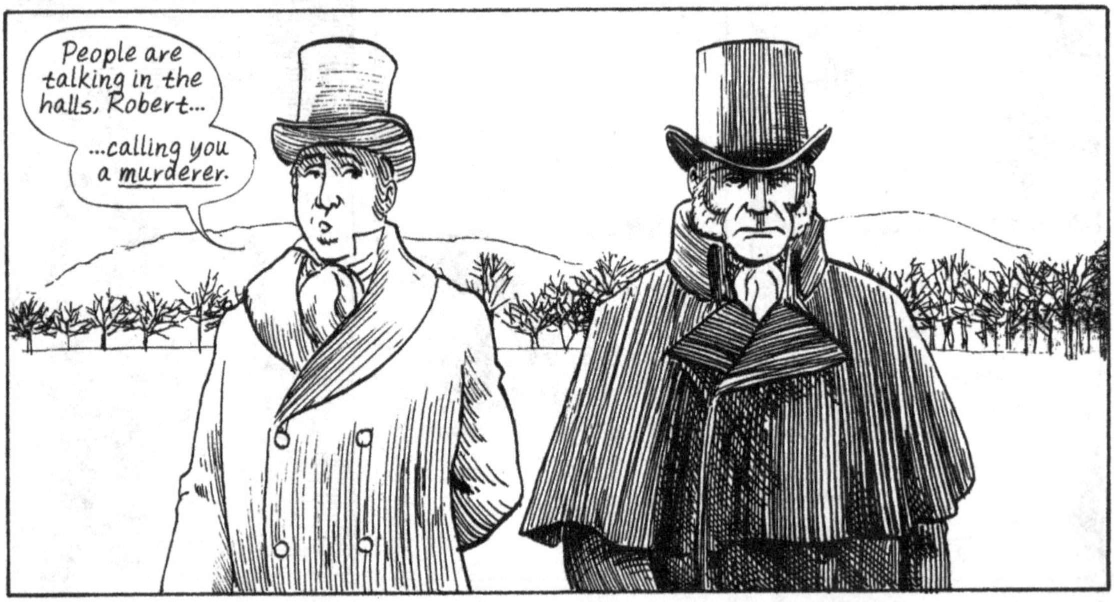

People are talking in the halls, Robert...
...calling you a murderer.

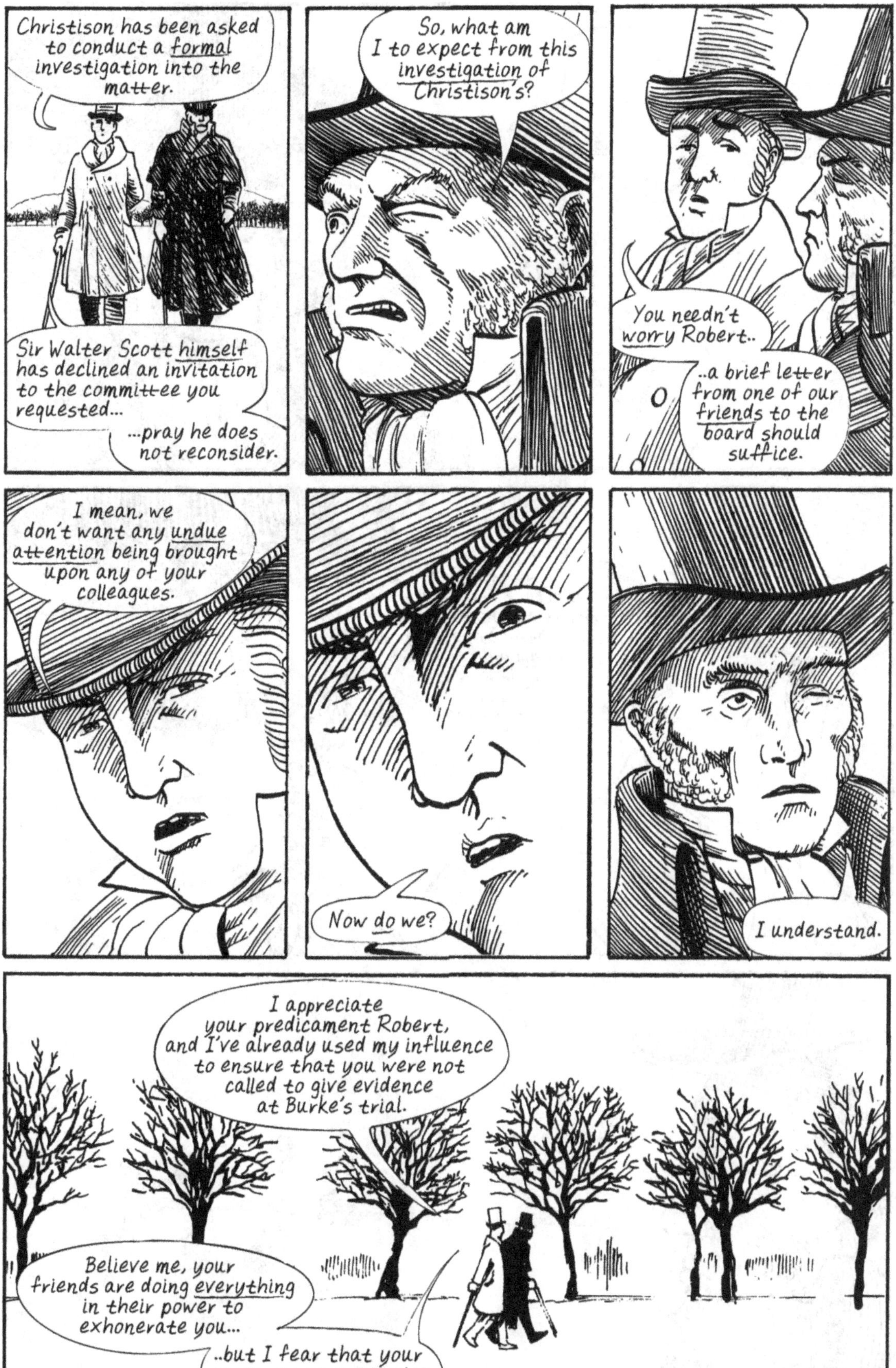
Christison has been asked to conduct a formal investigation into the matter.
Sir Walter Scott himself has declined an invitation to the committee you requested...
...pray he does not reconsider.
So, what am I to expect from this investigation of Christison's?
You needn't worry Robert..
..a brief letter from one of our friends to the board should suffice.
I mean, we don't want any undue attention being brought upon any of your colleagues.
Now do we?
I understand.
I appreciate your predicament Robert, and I've already used my influence to ensure that you were not called to give evidence at Burke's trial.
Believe me, your friends are doing everything in their power to exhonerate you...
..but I fear that your career as an anatomist in Edinburgh could soon turn sour.

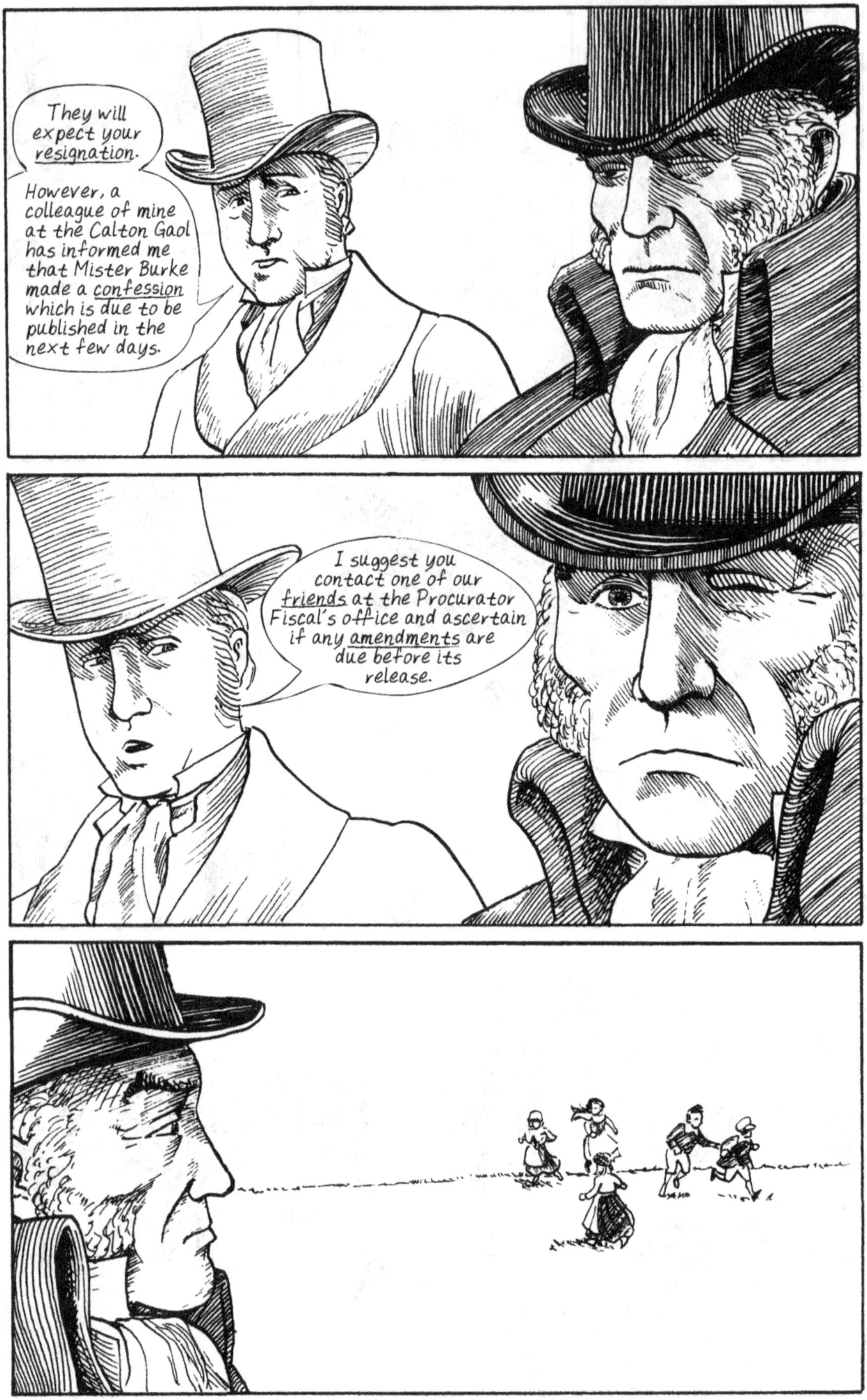
They will expect your resignation.
However, a colleague of mine at the Calton Gaol has informed me that Mister Burke made a confession which is due to be published in the next few days.
I suggest you contact one of our friends at the Procurator Fiscal's office and ascertain if any amendments are due before its release.

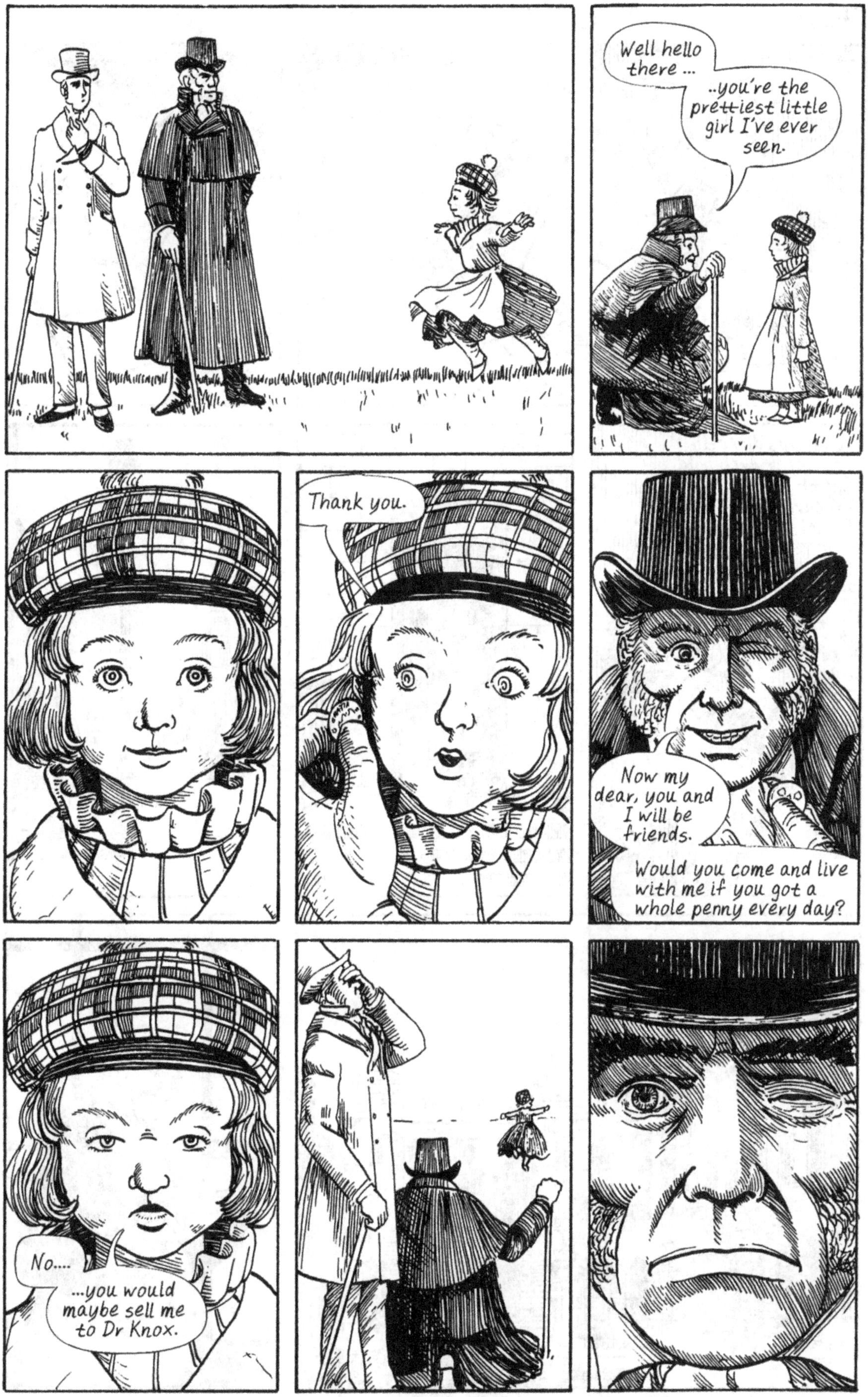
Well hello there ...
..you're the prettiest little girl I've ever seen.
Thank you.
Now my dear, you and I will be friends.
Would you come and live with me if you got a whole penny every day?
No....
...you would maybe sell me to Dr Knox.

Chapter Sixteen: Letters and Lies

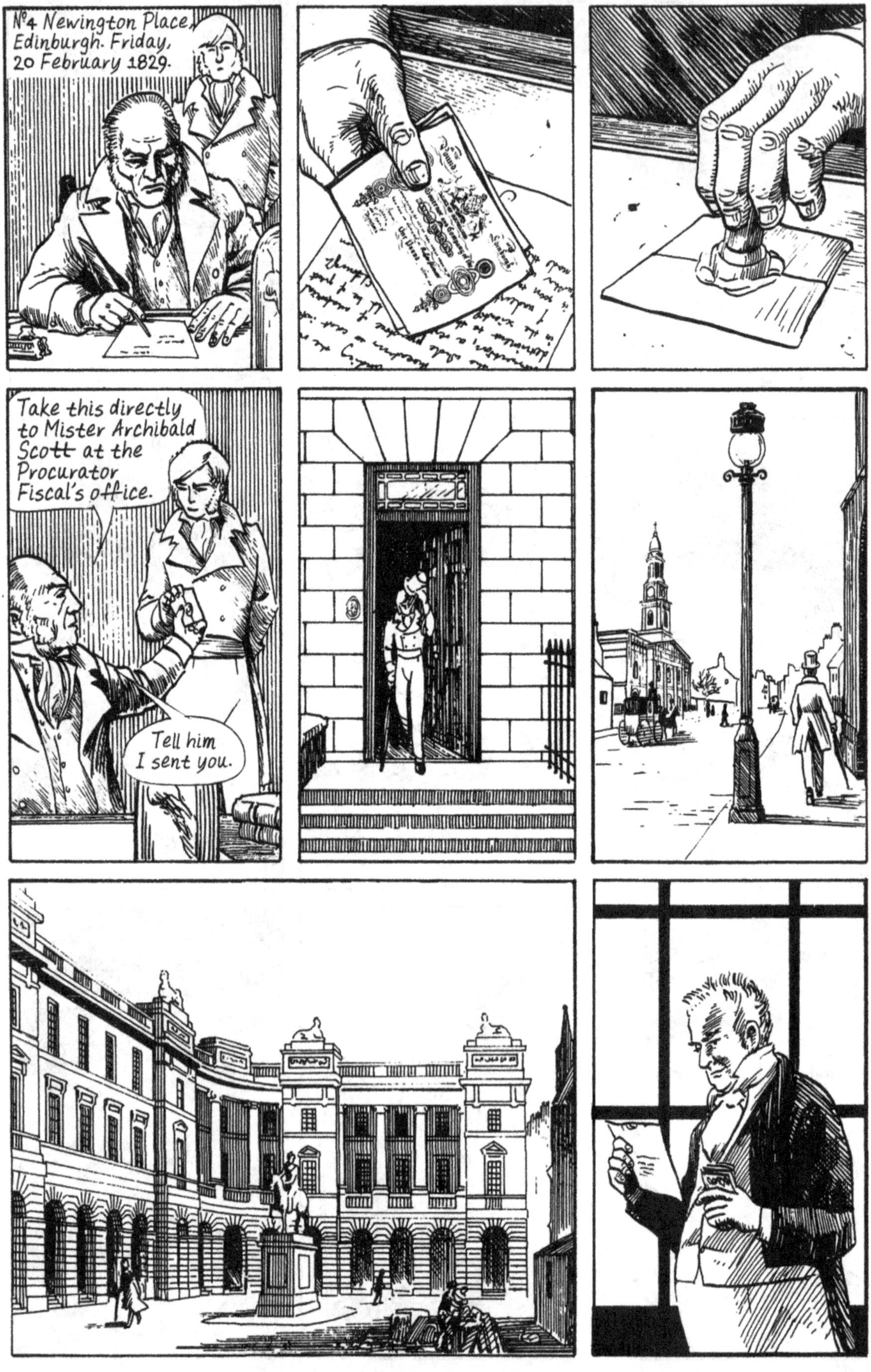
Nº4 Newington Place, Edinburgh. Friday, 20 February 1829.
Take this directly to Mister Archibald Scott at the Procurator Fiscal's office.
Tell him I sent you.

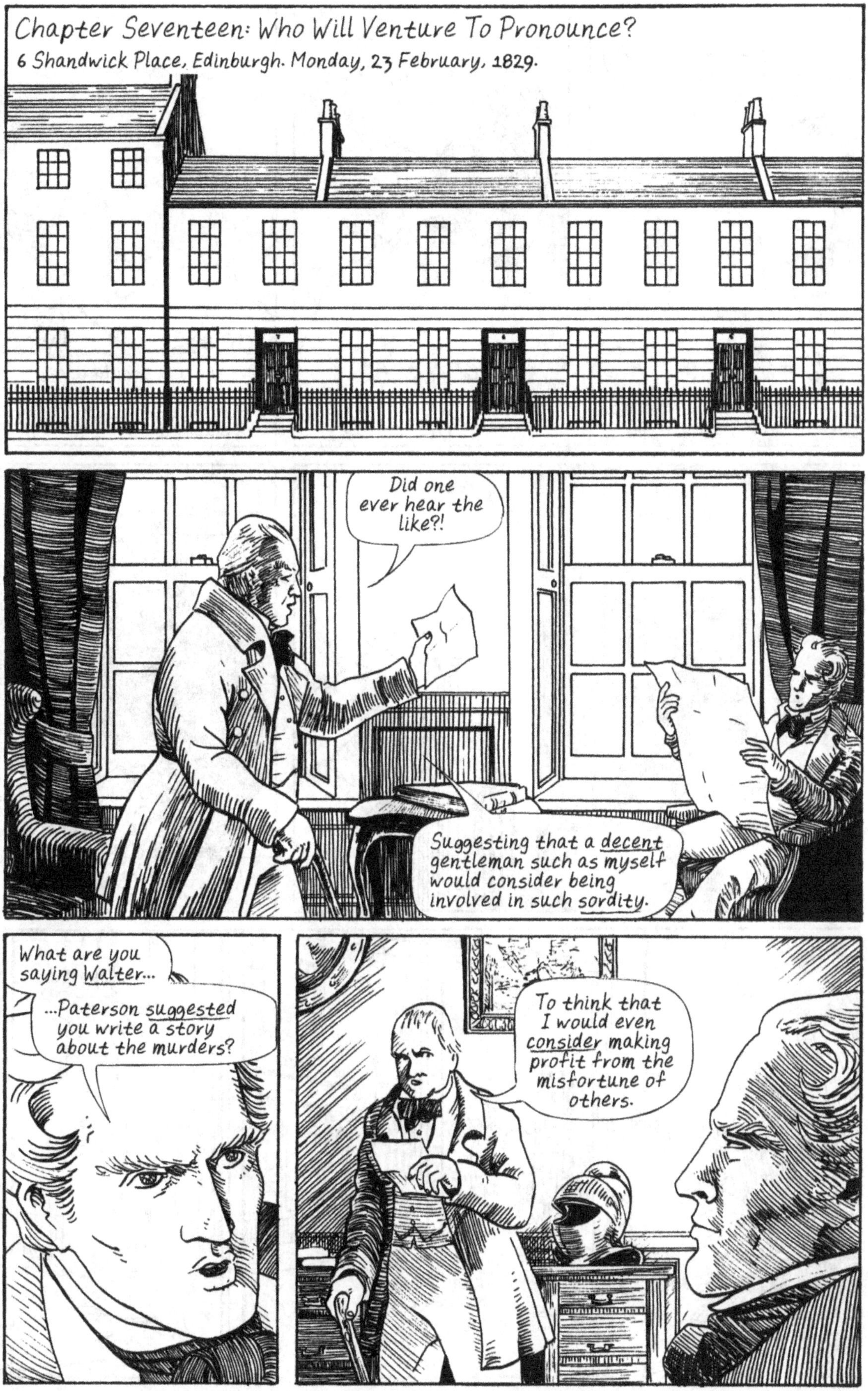
Chapter Seventeen: Who Will Venture To Pronounce?
6 Shandwick Place, Edinburgh. Monday, 23 February, 1829.
Did one ever hear the like?!
Suggesting that a decent gentleman such as myself would consider being involved in such sordity.
What are you saying Walter...
...Paterson suggested you write a story about the murders?
To think that I would even consider making profit from the misfortune of others.

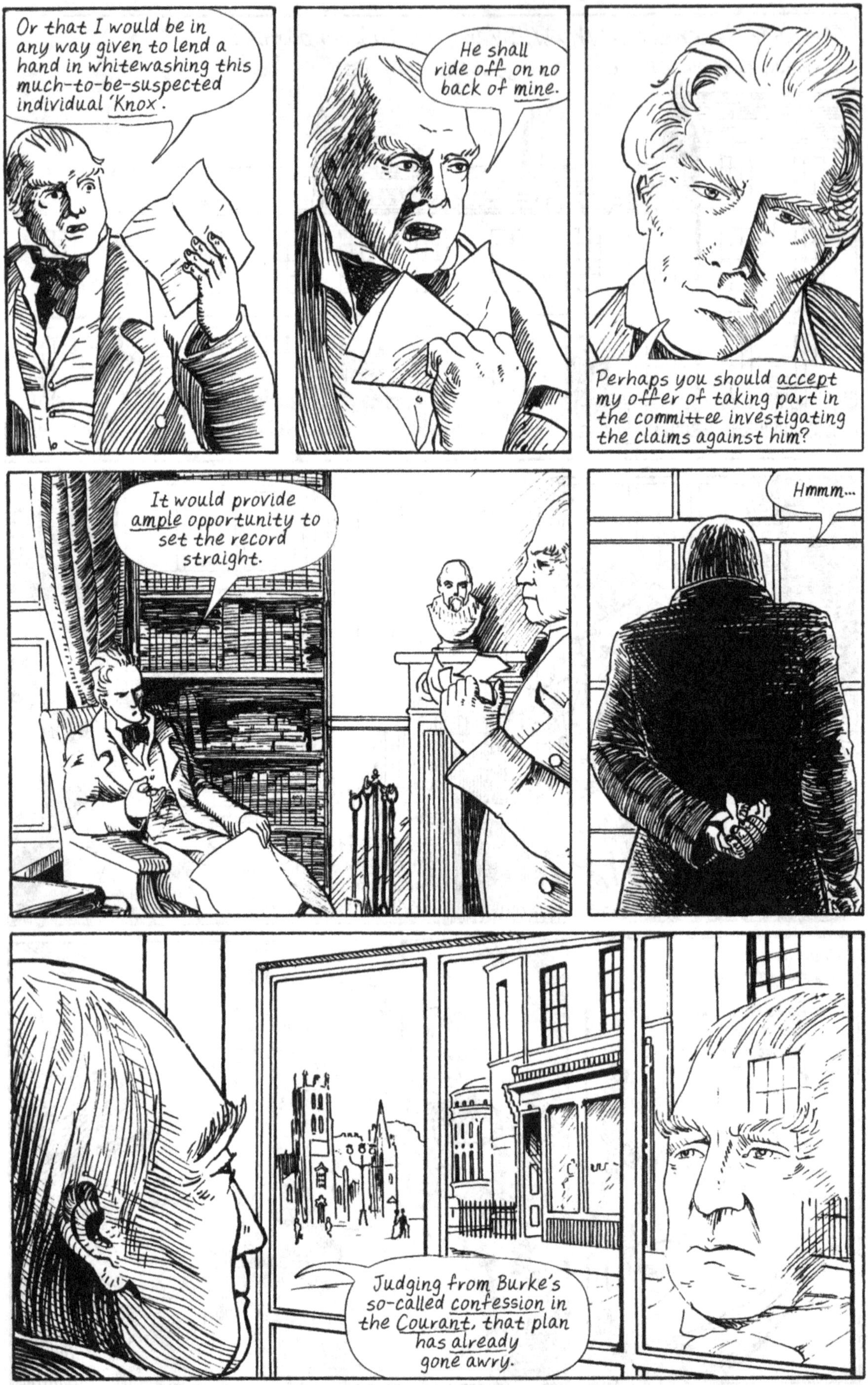
Or that I would be in any way given to lend a hand in whitewashing this much-to-be-suspected individual 'Knox'.
He shall ride off on no back of mine.
Perhaps you should accept my offer of taking part in the committee investigating the claims against him?
It would provide ample opportunity to set the record straight.
Hmmm...
Judging from Burke's so-called confession in the Courant, that plan has already gone awry.

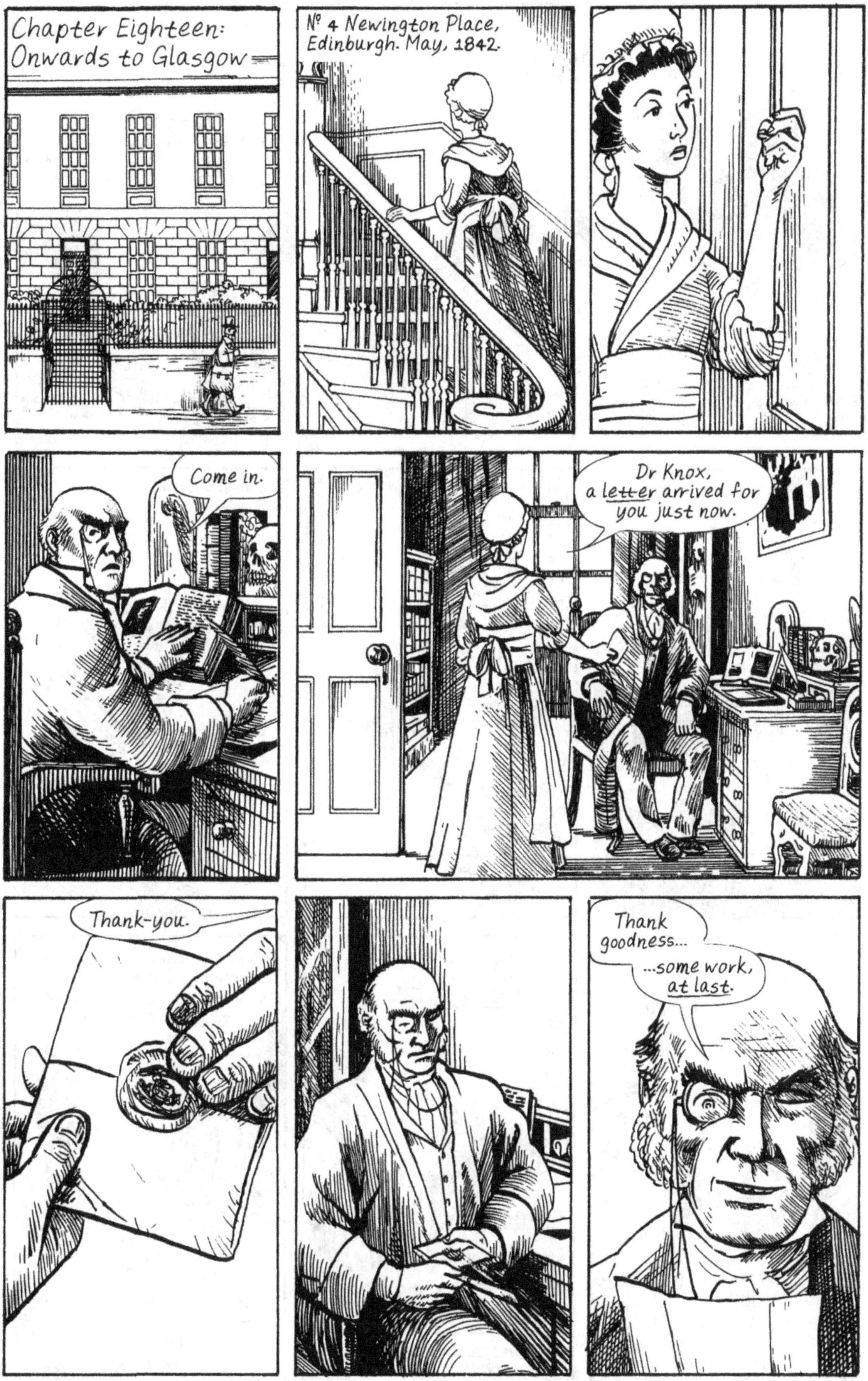
Chapter Eighteen: Onwards to Glasgow
Nº 4 Newington Place, Edinburgh. May, 1842.
Come in.
Dr Knox, a letter arrived for you just now.
Thank-you.
Thank goodness...
...some work, at last.

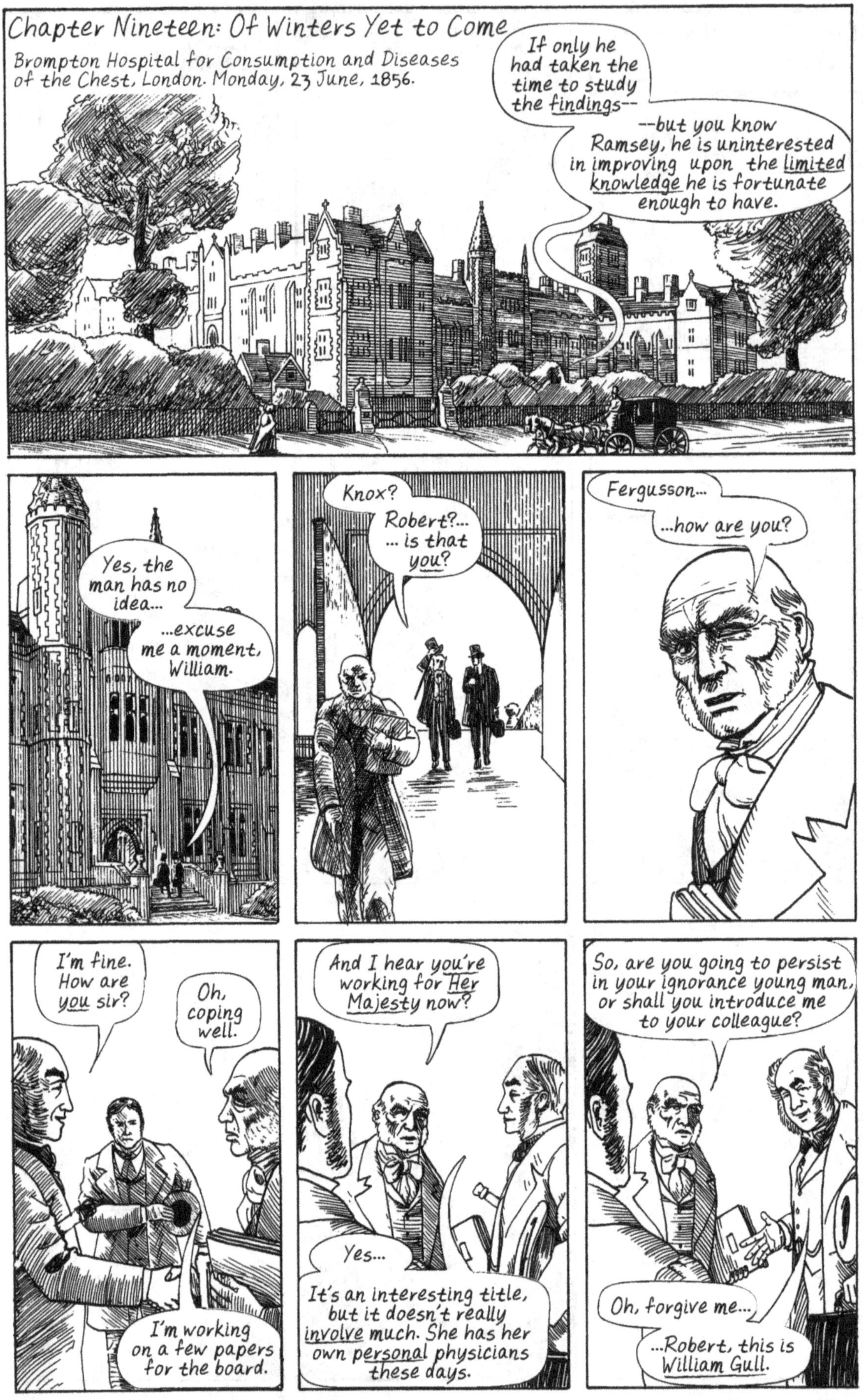

Chapter Nineteen: Of Winters Yet to Come
Brompton Hospital for Consumption and Diseases of the Chest, London. Monday, 23 June, 1856.
If only he had taken the time to study the findings--
--but you know Ramsey, he is uninterested in improving upon the limited knowledge he is fortunate enough to have.
Yes, the man has no idea...
...excuse me a moment, William.
Knox?
Robert?... ...is that you?
Fergusson...
...how are you?
I'm fine. How are you sir?
Oh, coping well.
I'm working on a few papers for the board.
And I hear you're working for Her Majesty now?
Yes...
It's an interesting title, but it doesn't really involve much. She has her own personal physicians these days.
So, are you going to persist in your ignorance young man, or shall you introduce me to your colleague?
Oh, forgive me...
...Robert, this is William Gull.

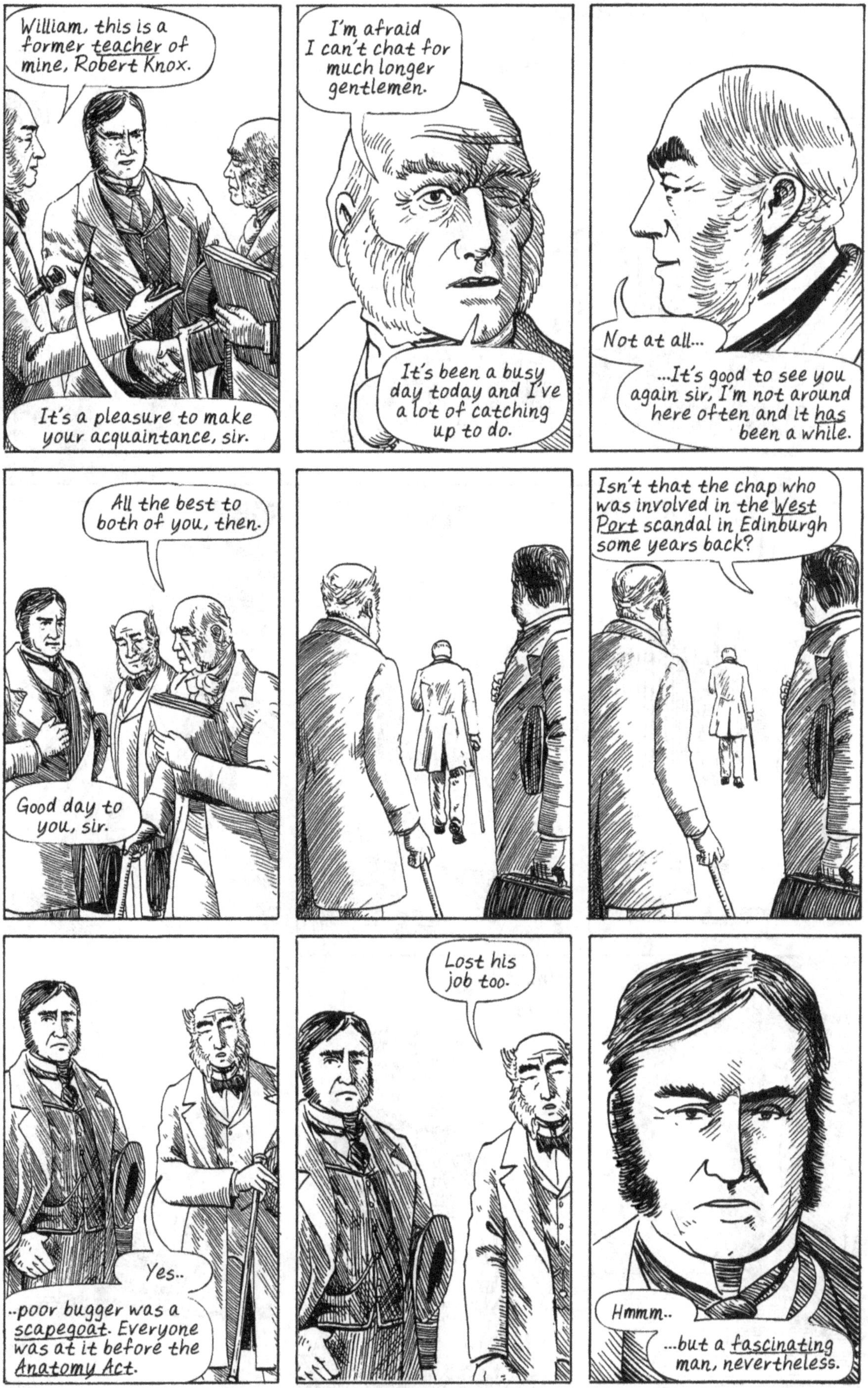
William, this is a former teacher of mine, Robert Knox.
It's a pleasure to make your acquaintance, sir.
I'm afraid I can't chat for much longer gentlemen.
It's been a busy day today and I've a lot of catching up to do.
Not at all...
...It's good to see you again sir, I'm not around here often and it has been a while.
All the best to both of you, then.
Good day to you, sir.
Isn't that the chap who was involved in the West Port scandal in Edinburgh some years back?
Yes..
..poor bugger was a scapegoat. Everyone was at it before the Anatomy Act.
Lost his job too.
Hmmm..
...but a fascinating man, nevertheless.

Epilogue: A Final Exchange

London, Oxford Street. Saturday, 31 August 1861.

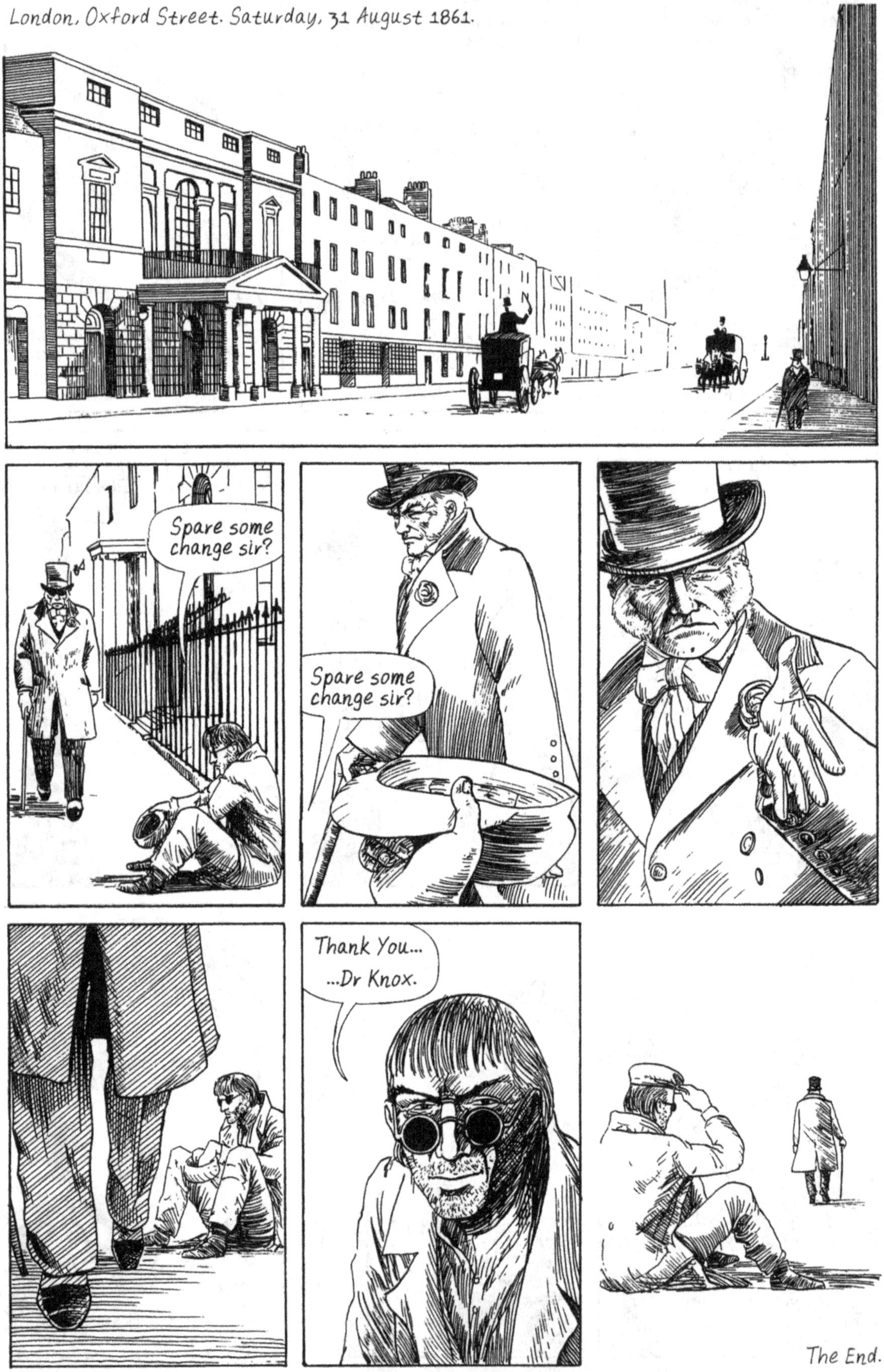
Spare some change sir?
Spare some change sir?
Thank You...
...Dr Knox.

The End.

Sined William Burke prisoner

APPENDIX

BURKE & HARE. APPENDIX.

Written By Martin Conaghan

The following notes give credit to any parts of the narrative of *Burke & Hare* that are based on fact, and, where possible, how I sourced the information. I have also indicated, where appropriate, fictionalised areas of the story.

These notes should not be considered a complete narrative or an exhaustive account of the Burke and Hare case; but more a companion to the story.

Burke & Hare was greatly influenced by Alan Moore and Eddie Campbell's magnificent *From Hell* (Top Shelf Productions, 1999) which attempted to solve the infamous 'Jack the Ripper' Whitechapel murders of 1888 by delving into the society in which the crimes were committed. However, *Burke & Hare* does not attempt to solve the crimes or analyse the behaviour of William Burke and William Hare, but merely to present the facts in as straightforward a fashion as possible, given the available historical and anecdotal information.

The majority of our story draws upon *Burke & Hare: The True Story* by Hugh Douglas (Robert Hale and Co. 1973); *Burke & Hare* by Owen Dudley Edwards (Polygon 1980); *Burke and Hare: The Year of The Ghouls* by Brian Bailey (Mainstream 2002) and *The Burke & Hare Crime Archive* by Alanna Knight (National Archives 2007) among other works listed in the bibliography towards the end of these notes.

Douglas and Edwards's reconstructions of the case saw me embark on a fascinating piece of research and enlightened me to the true facts of the Burke and Hare case (which is also known as *The West Port Murders* - after the area of West Port in Edinburgh where the crimes took place). While Edwards sets his reconstruction against the historical background of Edinburgh's Enlightenment, Douglas was probably the first writer since Henry Lonsdale in 1870 to imbue the story with a coherent and accessible narrative. Previous works, such as William Roughhead's *Burke and Hare* (Edinburgh and London: W. Hodge & Company, Ltd., 1921) tended to reconstruct the case from trial manuscripts, biographies and other official documents, but often failed to bind the tale together in any meaningful way.

The most recent books on the subject, from Brian Bailey, Allana Knight and the American historian Lisa Rosner - while offering some fresh arguments and insights regarding the finer points of the case, tend to repeat much that is already known about the story. However, they are worthy titles in their own right and Rosner's work has shed some new light on the case, which will be discussed later.

Prior to discovering the truth about Burke and Hare, my only recollection of the story was from my schooldays; where I had been given the false impression of an exaggerated fiction concerning graverobbers and ghouls.

However, the work presented here is not a tale of graverobbing. Neither is it an adaptation of the short story by Robert Louis Stevenson, *The Body-Snatcher* (which was only loosely based on the real events). *Burke & Hare* is a true story of cold-blooded murder, body-racketing in the medical establishment and ruthless greed.

CHAPTER ONE – In Which We Meet Mr Burke

PAGE 1

The scene depicted here is largely an invention and takes place exactly one week after William Burke's trial. No literature I have encountered details exactly how Burke summoned the Procurator Fiscal to his cell to make an official confession (the Procurator Fiscal is a Scottish legal figure similar to the District Attorney in the USA - essentially, the public prosecutor).

However, according to Hugh Douglas, Burke announced that he was ready to make a confession "after a week in the condemned cell" – Thursday 1 January, 1829 - and I am certain the guards at Calton

Gaol would have been displeased with Burke for disturbing them at any point on New Year's Day, due to the celebrations that usually take place the night before on Hogmanay.

William Burke and William Hare arrived in Edinburgh separately from Ireland in the years following the Napoleonic Wars, with hopes of securing gainful employment on the Union canal link between Glasgow and Edinburgh. Both Irish-born, Burke most likely from Urney (although Alanna Knight suggests he was from Strabane in Co. Tyrone; while others suggest 'Orrey', a place which doesn't exist) and Hare possibly from Newry - although little is actually known about Hare's place or date of birth. The pair somehow discovered each other, and the most notorious partnership in Scottish criminal history was soon forged.

Burke, and his common-law wife Nelly McDougal, persuaded Hare and his wife, Maggie Laird, to allow them to live rent-free at the lodging house, which Hare owned, at number 10 Tanner's Close. Over the next 12 months, the duo disposed of 17 individuals - 16 of whom were murdered - before finally being captured by the police on Saturday 1 November, 1828. The victims included 12 women, two men and two young boys – most of whom were plied with alcohol before being brutally smothered to death. The victims' bodies were then carried off to the lecture halls at number 10 Surgeons' Square, where they were sold to anatomist Dr Robert Knox, who dissected them in the name of medical science.

Burke's trial took place on Wednesday 24 December, 1828 and lasted only 24 hours; a timescale which would be virtually unheard of in a modern-day murder trial, but in 1828 was considered comprehensive. One so-called murder encyclopaedia I encountered in my research suggested that the date of 24 December was insignificant in 1828, since Christmas was not celebrated in Scotland at that time. In fact, Christmas has been celebrated in Scotland since before the modern tradition was popularised in the mid 1840s, although it was certainly on the wane in the early 1800s. The publication of Charles Dickens's *A Christmas Carol* in 1846 revived the festival as a holiday promoting charity and goodwill in the UK, along with Prince Albert Victor's introduction of the Christmas tree in about 1847. So, while the traditional Scottish holiday has always been New Year's Day, Scots have generally acknowledged the birth of Jesus in the appropriate Christian manner.

Stuart Beel's concept art for William Burke

The chief witnesses for the prosecution at Burke's trial were his murderous accomplice, William Hare, and Hare's wife Margaret; both of whom turned King's Evidence in return for immunity from the law. Remarkably, William Burke was only charged with three murders, despite having killed or participated in the murders at least 15 people - detailed throughout our narrative. (Note: Hare is alleged to have murdered one victim on his own – see the appendix to chapter six). However, since the authorities could link him to only three of the cases, and in the absence of two of the bodies, only one charge stood. The jury deliberated for just 50 minutes before reaching a guilty verdict, and the murderer Burke was sentenced to death by hanging.

Perhaps a week in his cold cell at Calton Gaol was enough to make Burke realise that the likelihood of his sentence being overturned was remote, if not impossible. He probably hoped that, by implicating Hare in a detailed confession, his accomplice would also be brought to justice. Sadly, this was not to be, and we will discuss later how Hare was given his freedom, as agreed in law.

Based on the information available to me, I have no reason to doubt the content of Burke's official confession, other than the strong attempts to implicate William and Margaret Hare in his crimes, which is entirely understandable given that both men had murdered in partnership; yet Hare escaped justice.

William Burke was ceremoniously executed on Monday 28 January, 1829 and his body was bequeathed to the medical faculty at Edinburgh University. More on this later.

PAGE 2

The first statement Burke makes on this page is probably the most important of the entire story; which is why I chose to start here.

The most common misconception about the Burke and Hare tale is that both men spent their time in graveyards digging up bodies for the purpose of selling them to dissectionists, or 'snatching' them from others who intended to do so. It follows that the pair subsequently resorted to murder to maintain a steady flow of fresh corpses, which is not supported by the facts.

'Resurrectionism' was the popular term applied to the practice of exhuming bodies from their recent burial plots to sell them to the medical establishment, and the practice which subsequently became known as 'bodysnatching' concerned the opportunist theft of corpses from resurrectionists.

However, Burke and Hare *murdered* all of their victims, with the exception of the first one; an old man named Donald who happened to die in Hare's lodging house at 10 Tanner's Close, allegedly owing his landlord rent money. Brian Bailey questions the value of Donald's debt to Hare in *Burke and Hare: The Year of the Ghouls*, but the point is moot. The old man's body was subsequently sold to Dr Robert Knox at 10 Surgeons' Square for £7 10s (seven pounds and ten shillings), and the lust for money soon consumed the two Irishmen.

Ironically, resurrectionism was not a crime in the 1800s, and both men would never have fallen foul of the law if graverobbing was their only enterprise; certainly, Burke would never have received the death penalty. Stealing a shroud or the death robes from a corpse, however, was a crime.

The reason for the widespread misapprehension about Burke and Hare's crimes can be broadly attributed to the Scottish writer Robert Louis Stevenson. Stevenson was born in 1850 and was a celebrity in his own lifetime, producing classic works such as *Kidnapped, Treasure Island* and *The Strange Case of Dr Jekyll and Mr Hyde*. He influenced the work of Ernest Hemingway, Rudyard Kipling, Vladimir Nabokov and J M Barrie, among others. In his short story *The Body-Snatcher*, (*Pall Mall Christmas Extra #13* Dec 1884), or *The Bodysnatchers*, depending on the publisher, Stevenson depicted characters similar to Burke and Hare who practised resurrectionism and illegally disposed of the disinterred bodies to medical research. The suitably chilling finale of the tale depicts the two horrified graverobbers unearthing the body of a man whom they know to have been previously dissected. Rumours of Burke and Hare's so-called graverobbing enterprises were widespread at the time of Burke's trial and for long afterwards. Stevenson's moderately successful fictionalised version of their story passed into the realm of public folklore, until 71 years later when it became the subject of the 1945 movie of the same name, directed by Academy Award winner Robert Wise and starring Boris Karloff and Bela Lugosi.

Subsequently, the tale assumed the popular shape it has today where the duo are miscast as graverobbing corpse thieves. Wise's movie is classic horror from the post-war era, featuring a chilling performance by Karloff as the graverobber/murderer John Gray; but it lacks period authenticity and the Scottish accents attempted by the cast are truly derisory. The least said about the recent effort from director John Landis, starring Simon Pegg and Andy Serkis, the better.

Several other writers and researchers have briefly chronicled their own versions of the Burke and Hare case; some with moderate accuracy, and others with startling inconsistency, often owing more to fiction than fact - or downright laziness. For example, *Historic South Edinburgh* by Charles J. Smith (Charles Skilton Ltd, 1978) states that Burke and Hare were "the Resurrectionists or body-snatching partnership who committed several murders in the Grassmarket and West Port area [of Edinburgh] and the exhuming of corpses in various Edinburgh graveyards". Jon E. Lewis, in his *Means To A Kill - An Encyclopaedia of Murder* (Headline Books, 1994) refers to Burke and Hare as "19th-Century graverobbers". The utterly dreadful and sensationalist *Fiendish Killers* by Anne Williams et al (Futura Books 2007) states that Burke and Hare "started off by simply robbing graves and selling the cadavers to doctors to use in their anatomy classes, but they thought that the digging late at night was too much like hard work." For some, it seems, the basic research of unearthing the facts is too much like hard work.

So, the portrayal of the West Port Murders in the wider media invariably perpetuates embellished tales of graverobbing and the re-animation of long-dead corpses, often to the point of parody. In 1985, Freddie Francis directed *The Doctor and The Devils*, a British movie based on an original screenplay by the Welsh poet Dylan Thomas that loosely dramatised the Burke and Hare story with Cockney-sounding actors and certain plot elements owing more to the *Carry On* films than factual research. The late Francis was a fine director and cinematographer, and I suspect his take on the story was an attempt to emulate the atmosphere he helped to create in David Lynch's 1980 film *The Elephant Man*. Perhaps, had he chosen to shoot his own movie in black and white, he may have achieved a similar effect. Despite some worthy attempts by Dylan to equate the tale with *MacBeth*, *The Doctor and The Devils* stands out as a remarkably dull film that passes itself off as a morality tale. Similarly, a 2004 *Doctor Who* audio drama featuring David Tennant in the role of Daft Jamie Wilson, makes the same fictional error of passing off Burke and Hare as a pair of graverobbers and a 1972 made-for-television effort by Vernon Sewell entitled *The Horrors of Burke and Hare*, veers so far into parody with a Chas n' Dave-style theme song that I found myself laughing out loud. The 1960 film *The Flesh and the Fiends* by John Gilling is somewhat closer to the mark, with Peter Cushing as Knox and Donald Pleasance as Hare. But film-makers and scriptwriters often find it difficult to resist the depiction of late-night graveyards and zombies. An entertaining diversion was Stephen Murphy's 1996 short film, *Burke and Hare the Musical*, featuring cleverly-crafted songs depicting the case, albeit irreverently. A recent BBC documentary revisiting the case also made a raft of basic research errors, including the number of victims, which I pointed out to the producers in advance of the broadcast date and was flatly dismissed.

So, the confession made by Burke on page two after his denouncement to the claims being made that he was a "resurrection-man" is fact and wholly supportable. Burke made his confession on Saturday 3 January, 1829, in his condemned cell at Calton Gaol in the presence of Mr George Tait, Sheriff-Substitute; Mr Archibald Scott, Procurator Fiscal; and Mr Richard J. Moxey, Assistant Sheriff-clerk.

On Thursday 22 January, 1829, in the presence of the same three people, with the addition of a Roman Catholic priest, Father William Reid, the confession was given what Hugh Douglas asserts as "every degree of authenticity" by Burke. At the second meeting, Burke confirmed his earlier confession and added additional details to the transcript, then signed the document.

Burke is alleged to have made *another* confession in the condemned cell the previous day, on Wednesday 21 January, to a journalist from the *Edinburgh Evening Courant* (subsequently, it became known as the 'Courant Confession') which appeared in the newspaper on 7 February, 1829 - following a protracted legal battle. (The official confession was also published in the Edinburgh Advertiser on 7 February). However, the Courant Confession adds little to the information provided by Burke in his official confession, and due to a restriction on page space in our narrative, I opted to avoid using it as a plot device and merged the days on which the two 'official' confessions took place - hence the presence of Father Reid throughout.

Stuart Beel's concept art for Dr Robert Knox

However, the Courant Confession receives further attention in a later appendix, as it features in our narrative towards the end of the story.

Despite the Courant Confession being authenticated by Burke's signature, mystery surrounds its origin, since Burke was not permitted any visitors to his cell (several people tried to bribe their way past the guards, and failed). I will discuss this aspect of the document in further detail later.

Owen Dudley Edwards states in the introduction to the second edition of *Burke & Hare* (Mercat Press 1993) that only *two* confessional statements were made in total by Burke in the condemned cell: the official confession on 3 January and the Courant Confession on 21 January - which is clearly an oversight on Edwards's part – either that, or he regards the statement on 22 January to be merely an extension of the official confession. Regardless,

two official meetings took place, and the individuals depicted here attended one, or both.

The next scene on page two depicts Burke commenting that Dr Robert Knox did not pay him for the body of Mary Docherty, the final victim; although her name is name is variously listed as, Doherty, Docherty and Campbell. The words uttered by Burke in this scene are based on information given in *Burke and Hare: The True Story*.

Dr Robert Knox was the eminent and quite brilliant anatomist who paid Burke and Hare handsomely for cadavers, which were then dissected, by him, in the name of medical science. Knox was born in Edinburgh in 1791 and studied at the Royal High School, before signing up to anatomy classes in 1810, which he failed.

Hugh Douglas states that Knox lived at 4 Newington Place in Edinburgh (whereas Charles J. Smith says Newington *Road*) and worked in partnership with his former teacher, Dr John Barclay, at 10 Surgeons' Square, where they both lectured in anatomy classes for the Royal College of Surgeons. Barclay was considered one of the greatest anatomists in Britain during the early 19th century, and fostered Knox's interest in medical science, in addition to teaching a young Charles Darwin, who later abandoned anatomy in favour of taxidermy. When Barclay retired from lecturing in 1821 due to ill health, his duties were assumed by Knox, who had been awarded a lifetime appointment as conservator of the college museum.

Before the arrests of William Burke, William Hare and their respective wives on Saturday 1 November, 1828, Robert Knox was viewed as one of the most popular anatomists in Edinburgh, if not the world. His field of expertise had expanded to incorporate zoology and included controversial racist views on anthropology. He was regarded by many as an engaging, enthusiastic speaker - despite sporting a dead left eye socket as a result of suffering smallpox as a child (earning him the nickname 'Old Cyclops') - dressing flamboyantly and presenting an air of authority. It seemed that nothing could halt the meteoric rise of his career as a medical professional - until he became acquainted with Burke and Hare. A simple matter of economics brought about the terrible practice of selling the dead to doctors in the early 1800s; the medical sciences were a growing and expensive form of education, and the lower classes had few means of generating income, other than heavy labour, prostitution or violent crime. Medical lecturers were being paid large sums by hundreds of anatomy students eager to further their knowledge, and there were many who sought to profit from the deceased in order to advance the discipline and their pockets.

Medical lecturers required a fresh supply of cadavers in order to carry out their work, but were permitted only a limited supply for their lectures, all too infrequently provided by the hangman. The Murder Act of 1742 stipulated that only the bodies of hanged murderers could be donated for dissection, so fresh corpses were in high demand. Therefore, many surgeons often resorted to the dissection of animals or the procurement of bodies via immoral or illegal means, such as bodysnatching. Pressure from the medical establishment relaxed the laws somewhat, allowing scientists to dissect the bodies of suicide victims, orphans and unclaimed dead persons. But the number of donated bodies were few and far between. As a result, a trade in body thefts sprung up around Britain's prominent medical establishments, and the resurrectionist trade experienced something of a gold rush.

Burke's reasons for mentioning that Knox had not paid him for the body of the Docherty woman are also allegedly true, according to Hugh Douglas. Burke wanted the fee in order to purchase clothing so that he could appear respectable in public at his execution. The relative narrative on page two is a contrivance of events detailed by Hugh Douglas and does not form part of Burke's official confession - which brings me back to the Courant Confession. Since Burke never received his fee from Dr Knox for the body of the Docherty woman - or the new clothing he required - I find it unlikely that he would offer a fresh confession to a newspaper without the return of favour in some form; perhaps the new clothing he desired, unless his intention was solely to implicate Hare. To be clear, Burke was an unscrupulous character, a murderer who profited from the sale of his victims' corpses - which leads me to believe that the Courant Confession was probably the work of an enterprising individual at Caton Gaol or the Procurator Fiscal's office, and in all likelihood was not initiated or generated by Burke himself.

In the harsh economic climate of 1829, few would have ignored the opportunity to profit from the much-publicised Burke and Hare case - and many did - with several 'official' Burke confessions appearing in newspapers almost every other day. I suspect it would have been a simple matter of copying a version of the original document and forging Burke's signature, then selling it on to the Courant at a later date. On the other hand, perhaps a junior clerk (or a senior official) at the PF's office was bribed by a representative of Dr Knox to make additions to the confession which would vindicate the good doctor of any involvement in the murders. Knox was widely suspected of involvement in the West Port crimes and Burke's 'new' confession could have been surreptitiously released to the newspapers, passing it off as an authentic document after the accused had been executed and, therefore, incapable of refuting its content. I present this hypothesis because the Courant Confession ends with a brief passage which strikes the reader as the only new information in the document, where Burke vehemently denies that Dr Knox or his assistants had any influence in, or prior knowledge of, the murders. If indeed this fanciful conspiracy was how the Courant Confession was originated, it did very little in the way of shifting the blame from Knox, as we will discuss in a later appendix.

Despite my somewhat sceptical views of the Courant Confession, Owen Dudley Edwards is almost certain that it is authentic, and bases much of his debate on its content. Undeniably, the Courant Confession seems to elicit detailed information which would probably have been difficult to invent, such as a lengthy account of Hare's horse refusing to carry one of the dead bodies beyond the Edinburgh meal-market; which is interpreted by many biographers as a superstitious phenomenon. However, much of the narrative contains flowery prose, suggesting the work of an educated mind, and perhaps was extrapolated from details redacted from the official confession. According to Owen Dudley Edwards, it is well established that trial manuscripts and official court documents of the era were often amended by lawyers following lengthy trials before publication or insertion into any official collection, in order that foolish remarks could be altered for public scrutiny.

PAGE 3

Burke opens his confession by taking us back about one year and describes the events which led himself and William Hare to commit murder. He goes back as far as "the Hallow-fair before last", which was Halloween; 31 October 1827.

PAGE 4

First comes the tale of an old man named Donald who died in Hare's lodging house at 10 Tanner's Close owing rent money, and whose body was sold to Dr Robert Knox for £7 10s. The words used by Burke in our narrative are taken almost verbatim from his official confession. According to Owen Dudley Edwards, the biographer Henry Lonsdale in *A Sketch of the Life and Writings of Robert Knox the Anatomist* (London: Macmillan, 1870) fixed the date of old Donald's case as 29 November. The famous Scottish lawyer and amateur criminologist William Roughead, in his book *Burke and Hare* (Edinburgh and London: W. Hodge & Company, Ltd. 1921), suggests that Lonsdale may have had access to Robert Knox's records, which would help support this. I have avoided mentioning a precise date, since it bears little relevance to the narrative at this stage.

In the flashback panels on page four, Burke and Hare are depicted seeking directions from a student at the Edinburgh University college yard. The eagle-eyed readers among you should recognise the student as a very young Charles Darwin, who was a medical student at Edinburgh University until he dropped out late in 1827. According to financial accounts detailing Darwin's student bills published in 2009, he left Edinburgh in 1827 and arrived in Cambridge on 26 January, 1828 to take up studies at Christ's College in Cambridge. I have inserted Darwin in this scene for fanciful purposes, as it is entirely possible that he was still residing in Edinburgh around the time that Burke and Hare were attempting to sell old Donald's body. It is also likely that Darwin would have attended at least one of Knox's lectures on anatomy at some stage in his ill-fated career as an anatomist, and he would undoubtedly have been aware of the location of Knox's well-known residence. Certainly, it is established fact that Darwin attended lectures given by Knox's predecessor, Dr John Barclay.

Burke also mentions in this scene - and in his official confession - that Dr Knox examined Donald's body before payment was arranged, but did not ask where Burke and Hare had obtained the corpse. If Knox *did* examine Donald's body upon delivery, it seems likely that Burke and Hare would have met him on this particular occasion. Hugh Douglas reprints Burke's entire confession at the end of his book, yet fails to note this. Instead, Douglas places the first meeting of Burke and Hare with Dr Robert Knox later in their killing spree. Douglas goes on to say that after Donald's body had been sold, Burke and Hare subsequently murdered a man known as 'Joseph the miller', then proceeded to dispose of an old woman named Abigail Simpson, whereupon "for the first time, they met the great anatomist, Robert Knox".

CHAPTER TWO - A Woman From Gilmerton

PAGES 5-12

The visualised allurement and murder of Abigail Simpson depicted in these pages is based on the available facts, although, the actual visualisation of the event is largely an invention for story purposes. For the benefit of non-Scots readers "saut" is an aberration of "salt".

The song featured on page seven is entitled *The Jolly Beggar-Man,* and has been in circulation since the early 18th Century. I thought it fitting to have Burke and Hare singing an Irish ballad, since both men hailed from the Emerald Isle. Thanks are due to my former colleague Margaret McCabe for offering the suggestion and providing the lyrics and music to the song for the purposes of our story. Abigail Simpson's phrase at the bottom of page eight, "just the one", is taken from the title of Graham Lord's biography of the writer and journalist Jeffrey Bernard. As Mr Pickering pointed out to me, 'one' is never just 'one', and poor old Abigail's fondness for a drink probably contributed to her chilling demise.

Abigail Simpson was lured back to Hare's lodgings for a drink and spent the night there after falling unconscious. She was smothered by the duo in the morning, having suffered from a serious hangover beforehand, with Hare the main instigator, according to Burke's official confession. Burke referred to Abigail in his official confession as "a woman from Gilmerton", Gilmerton being an area of Edinburgh. The Courant Confession gives her name as Abigail Simpson and Burke himself placed the murder as being in the Spring, whereas Hugh Douglas and the Courant Confession both insist it took place in February. My views on the Courant Confession are already obvious, and I have disagreed one these pages simply to be contrary. For the purposes of our story, I have suggested that the murder took place in March, since March is nearer to Spring than February.

Exactly how these two men could steel themselves to kill a helpless and harmless old woman is completely beyond comprehension, and my reasons for visualising the murder in these pages are quite simple; in my opinion it was the first of the 16 murders, and it was a most cold-blooded start to their campaign of utter evil.

Owen Dudley Edwards continually expresses an affinity with William Burke in his very extensive *Burke & Hare* - almost certainly based on his shared Irish roots - and extends his admiration to describing the "likeability" of the man. By most accounts, Burke was a friendly, educated character who enjoyed a song, a dance and a joke. However, his partnership with Hare inhumanely ended the lives of at least 15 innocent human beings (allegedly, Hare killed one of the victims by himself - see the appendix to page 19) and regardless of any redeeming personality features, Burke was a cold-blooded, calculating murderer and certainly not an individual to be revered or trusted.

Make no mistake, Burke and Hare's actions were not the work of a couple of loveable Irish rogues - they were murderers: devious, cruel and without conscience. In comparison, Hugh Douglas describes the pair as "fiends out of Hell" and Sir Robert Peel, the founder of the Metropolitan Police, described the West Port murders as exceeding "any thing in horror of which I ever heard". Few would disagree with their assessments.

Edwards also neglects that the majority of Burke and Hare's victims were women or youths and dismisses the demonization of the pair as an attempt by biographers to define their actions. In truth, both were dangerous, untrustworthy men and it is entirely remiss to overestimate the "likeability" of anyone who behaves in such a cruel, evil fashion towards their fellow human beings. I firmly believe that, had Edwards been alive at the time of the West Port Murders, he would have been thoroughly outraged by the terrible events of 1828.

In terms of their modus operandi, Burke and Hare are generally not viewed in the same light as serial killers of the 20th and 21st centuries, who tend to excuse themselves from the rules of society in order to brutalise and dehumanise their victims. However, the duo's methods achieved the same outcome; they consciously lured innocent people into situations where they could brutally murder their victims with impunity. The corpses of their victims suffered the ultimate indignity of dissection and the denial of a proper burial or cremation.

As mentioned in the appendix to page four, in his narrative, Hugh Douglas places the murder of Joseph the miller first and the murder of Abigail Simpson second. However, Burke's confession clearly lists the Simpson woman first and Joseph second. Even the dubious Courant Confession does not place the murders in such an order; Abigail Simpson comes first on the Courant's list, and Joseph the miller comes seventh. I cannot fathom Douglas's reasons for doing this. He baffles the reader further towards the end of his book with a chronological list of the murders, based on Burke's official confession, which depicts the murder of Joseph the miller *after* Abigail Simpson. One of his reasons for suggesting that Joseph the miller was murdered before Abigail Simpson is that it seems "the more logical sequence"; Joseph had been lodging at Hare's house, and was evidently suffering from what appeared to be a contagious and terminal illness. Therefore, Douglas suggests that Joseph was murdered first because a sick man posed a threat to Hare's lodging income, making it "a single, simple step from the case of old Donald to help Joseph on his way". He qualifies the assertion by pointing out that Joseph was not tempted into 10 Tanner's Close, was not plied with alcohol and, therefore, his murder differed from the modus operandi of the other murders; so it probably came first.

Both Owen Dudley Edwards and Hugh Douglas support Sir Walter Scott's claims of having viewed William Hare's long-disappeared confession, which apparently proves Douglas' assessment of the inconsistent order of the murders (for more on Sir Walter Scott, see the appendix to page 55). Evidently, Scott confirmed that the same murder list, with a varying sequence, was proffered separately by both Burke and then later by Hare in his King's Evidence statement. However, Douglas fails to quote Sir Walter Scott directly, where Owen Dudley Edwards does, yet Douglas asserts that Hare (in a statement which mysteriously vanished and has never been found in almost two centuries) confirmed that Joseph the miller was indeed the first victim to be murdered, and not Abigail Simpson. I cannot substantiate Douglas's hypothesis, although I do not doubt Sir Walter Scott's assessment of the murder sequence, and have therefore decided to base the order of the murder list on Burke's official confession; where Abigail Simpson is killed first and Joseph second. Even Owen Dudley Edwards suggests that Abigail Simpson was "one of the earliest victims".

CHAPTER THREE - The Sale of the Century

PAGES 13-15

Here we see Burke and Hare meeting a porter at the foot of Edinburgh Castle who had been dispatched to meet them by Alexander Miller, one of Knox's assistants. The porter then leads them to 10 Surgeons' Square, where they meet Dr Robert Knox and sell him the body of Abigail Simpson. The events depicted are taken from Burke's official confession. Despite my previous argument (at the end of the appendix to page 4) I thought it would be simpler for the *reader* to first meet Knox on this occasion, since this was the first of the murders to be visualised in our account of the case.

The remaining events depicted on these two pages are based entirely on Burke's official confession, with two exceptions: the fee of £10 agreed by Knox is taken from the Courant Confession, and the parting statement made by Alexander Miller to the two men was made on the occasion of Burke and Hare's *first* visit to Surgeons' Square, when they sold the body of old Donald. It has been included on this occasion for story purposes, and is taken from Burke's official confession.

CHAPTER FOUR - The Lovely Month of May

PAGES 16-17

As mentioned previously, Burke goes on to discuss the murder of Joseph the miller in these pages, and continues by cataloguing the murders of "an old woman" in May, 1828; "an Englishman soon afterwards", "an old woman named Haldane" (more of whom later), "a cinder woman"; and "about Midsummer, a woman, with her grandson".

The singularly repeated statement "disposed of in the same manner" is taken verbatim from Burke's confession, and in all likelihood was probably not uttered by Burke as often as it is here or during his actual confession session. I suspect it was one of the clerical abbreviations referred to by Owen Dudley Edwards and, in all probability, was applied by the individual who transcribed the details. Much of Burke's dialogue in the confession scenes throughout our narrative is taken directly from his official confession (or, occasionally from the Courant Confession, if it suits the purposes of our story), and does not necessarily reflect the actual words spoken by Burke at the time. However, I suspect that Burke, being a reasonably well-educated man, probably affected an air of polite aloofness in the presence of the Procurator Fiscal in order to appear more intelligent – hence the change from Irish brogue in the main scenes, to an affected tone of politeness during his confessional statement scenes.

The murders themselves need no further explanation as they are recounted exactly as Burke listed them in his confession. However, on page 42 a small, necrotic-looking boy holding a hangman's noose is visualised in a confusing nightmare sequence, so the murder of the "woman, with her grandson" requires further clarification.

The boy's murder was of such a brutal and sadistic nature, that when I read Hugh Douglas's account of the event, I was deeply shocked by it. According to Douglas, Burke had been out roaming the streets looking for a potential victim, when he encountered an old man who was completely inebriated. He successfully persuaded the man to come back to the lodging house at Tanner's Close for a drink, and both men set about making their way back when Burke encountered a woman and her grandson.

Burke abandoned the old man, and instead concentrated on the woman - which raises a startling curiosity, suggesting a potential sexual motive in the murders; the old man was alone and therefore much more vulnerable, he was also very drunk and presumably an easy kill. Burke's new target of *two* people would have proven formidable, so why did he change his plans? Could it be that he anticipated a greater profit margin for delivering two bodies to Knox? Was it a sexual urge? Despite these questions, I am unaware of any evidence which points to sexual violation in any of the murders, and I abandon the notion here; although Burke's sexual advances to another victim, Mary Paterson, are covered in the appendix notes to pages 20-25.

Broggan's house, seen from the rear

Douglas asserts that once back at Tanner's Close, Burke and Hare plied the woman with alcohol until she fell asleep in the lodging room. Nelly McDougal (Burke's wife) and 'Lucky' Hare (Hare's common-law wife) distracted the woman's deaf-mute grandson while Burke and Hare smothered the woman to death. Following her murder, and after much debate over the boy's future, the group decided that he should die also, and without warning, Burke put the boy over his knee and broke his back.

The bodies were pronounced satisfactory by Dr Knox's assistants and the two men were paid the standard 'Summer rate' of £8 for each.

Apparently, Burke was gravely disturbed by his actions on this occasion and he experienced frequent nightmares about the murder, often sleeping with a lit candle and a bottle of whisky by his bedside.

Owen Dudley Edwards analyses this particular

murder at length, labelling it "the case of the broken back", referencing several narrators and asserting in no uncertain terms that the murder did not take place in such a fashion and was definitely a myth. Allana Knight suggests that a corpse with a broken back would have raised concerns at 10 Surgeons' Square, but spinal injuries are not always apparent and by Burke's admission, the bodies were stuffed into a herring barrel, so would have undoubtedly been bruised and bashed during transportation to Surgeons' Square. However, I can find no evidence to suggest that the boy *did not* suffer at the hands of Burke in such a horrific fashion, even if the murder does fall out of line with the modus operandi of the previous victims. So, I have avoided visualising the actual crime in the narrative. However, as previously stated, I have inserted a nightmare sequence on page 42, which is obviously fiction and open to interpretation.

CHAPTER FIVE - The Long Road Home

PAGE 18

The scene depicted here is allegedly true and has been entered because of a lack of details in the official confession. Burke made no mention of the incident in his confession, but detailed the events in the Courant Confession.

According to various narrators, the old woman depicted was found by the police sitting on a stairwell, drunk and incapable. One of the policemen happened to be Burke's neighbour, Andrew Williamson, who was simply relieved to be rid of the old drunkard and allowed to go about his work. The woman was subsequently murdered by Burke and Hare, and then taken to Knox's rooms at Surgeons' Square - and if the Courant Confession is to be believed – the pair received £10 pounds for her body.

Personally, I find the fees in the Courant Confession to be somewhat suspicious. Based on the information given, the prices do not reconcile with the fees agreed between the murderous duo and Dr Robert Knox. Hugh Douglas asserts that two separate fees were arranged by Knox with Burke and Hare for bodies procured; a 'Winter fee' when bodies were in greater demand, and a lesser 'Summer fee' when they were not. Owen Dudley Edwards states this arrangement was probably due to storage problems in the summer. However, the medical cadavers were often stored in alcohol, which would have been available all year round, so the reason for a varying fee was probably because of a fall in attendance at lectures during summer months. The notices for Knox's anatomy and physiology lectures, posted on 25 September 1828, specified a start date of 4 November, and the end date for the lectures in practical anatomy and operative surgery was given as "the end of July 1829".

The Courant Confession states that the 'Summer fee' of only £8 was given for the bodies of the "woman and her grandson", yet the woman taken from the police earned Burke and Hare £10. The old woman and her grandson were apparently murdered and disposed of in June, whereas the woman taken from the police is mentioned later in both confessions, indicating that it was probably around July or August - which is still Summer, albeit beyond the date of Knox's lectures and the Scottish weather notwithstanding. Fortunately, these frequent irregularities and inconsistencies in the Courant Confession provide me with even more ammunition to further debunk the document. However, it does not prevent me from contriving its content for fictional purposes. In any case, Burke and Hare's murder spree lasted about nine months from the first to last victim, and saw them profit from the demise of 17 unfortunate souls, 16 of whom were killed in cold blood.

CHAPTER SIX - Ladies For Sale

PAGE 19

The details on this page are taken verbatim from Burke's confession. Remarkably, Burke and Hare even managed to murder and dispose of the *daughter* of the woman named Haldane (mentioned in the appendix to page 17) just as easily as they had her mother. Burke goes on to describe the murder of the Paterson girl, which is further detailed in the next appendix. The grotesque-looking character in panel four is John Broggan, the owner of the lodging house where Burke was living at the time of the Haldane woman's murder (by most accounts, Burke and Hare were somewhat peripatetic, although never strayed further than the confines of Edinburgh city for more than a few days at a time). According to various biographers, Hare's decision to murder and dispose of a body by himself in Burke's absence caused a split between the duo, and Burke moved to Broggan's house with his common-law wife for a short spell. Broggan's facial deformity was present from birth, but was exacerbated by burns suffered in a fire. A wax model of the man's face is on display at Surgeons' Hall in Edinburgh – if you are ever in Edinburgh, pop along and have a look, it's disturbingly captivating. Mr Pickering couldn't resist including such a monstrosity in the story, and went to the trouble of re-drawing the panel to serve the man's hideous visage the justice it deserves.

CHAPTER SEVEN - A Thing Of Rare Beauty

PAGES 20-25

The murder and disposal of Mary Paterson is probably the most important of all the murders in the Burke and Hare case, since more is known about it than any of the others, with the exception of the case of 'daft' Jamie Wilson and the final victim, Mary Docherty (Burke was convicted on the evidence surrounding the final murder). Astute readers will notice that the date sequence in this particular flashback scene is out of sequence with the previous visualisations. This is intentional, and is based on the sequence given by Burke in his official confession. In the previous scene on page 18, Burke is depicted feigning a recollection of Mary Paterson's murder - which took place on Wednesday 9 April (as if he would be likely to forget it). Burke's dialogue in this scene is an invention on my part. Alanna Knight states that the Paterson murder took place on Wednesday 12 April 1828. However, 12 April fell on a Saturday in 1828. The date of Wednesday 9 April is taken from Hugh Douglas's *Burke & Hare: The True Story*, but has no basis in fact, since no specific date is given in Burke's Official Confession or the Courant Confession other than "in the month of April".

Mary Paterson is described by various authors as a prostitute who was well-known around the streets of Edinburgh's Old Town, and after her body was sold to Knox's assistants, it was purportedly preserved in whisky for many months afterwards. Her voluptuous form and striking beauty were commented on by many students of Robert Knox, who apparently viewed her corpse during lectures on muscular tone and development. Her lifeless form was also illustrated, somewhat perversely, by J. Oliphant.

The visualised events leading up to her death and the subsequent sale of her body to Knox's assistants are an elaboration of the account given by Hugh Douglas in Burke and Hare: The True Story, as is the incident between Burke and his common-law wife Helen McDougal. On page 24, Burke and Hare are seen carrying Paterson's body in a sack and find themselves accosted by a group of children who seem to have figured out that the package being transported is a dead body. This is taken from Hugh Douglas's *Burke & Hare: The True Story*. In my original script, I had depicted the pair walking along West Port with Paterson's body, but as Will pointed out to me, Burke awas living with Constantine Burke – his brother - at the time, so we agreed to change the setting to St Mary's Wynd, which is a more appropriate route for the duo to have taken on their way to 10 Surgeon's Square. As with all of the depictions of Edinburgh's streets in 1828, Will's reconstruction of the locale, its structures, people and places is so vivid, you can almost taste the air of the back streets.

Hugh Douglas states that Paterson's body was still warm when Burke and Hare delivered her to Surgeons' Square and that the two men were subsequently asked several questions about its origin. However, Burke maintains in his official confession that he could recall of no remarks from those present about the body being warm, and that the pair had no dealings with Knox on this occasion.

Before payment was made, the duo were supposedly

given a pair of scissors and ordered to cut off Paterson's hair, possibly because she had been recognised by one of the students and could be identified by many more. However, in the charcoal sketches of her made by Oliphant, her hair is intact - which could just be artistic license, but at least renders the assertion questionable. That she was a prostitute suggests she would have been familiar to many of the young medical students who attended Knox's lectures – in fact, Owen Dudley Edwards pursues the notion that she was romantically involved with one of Knox's students, William Fergusson, who went on to become Sergeant-Surgeon to Queen Victoria and died in 1877. Edwards proffers that it was Fergusson who recognised the body of Mary Patterson upon her delivery to Knox. However, since I have unearthed no such proof of the alleged relationship between the two, I have instead depicted a nondescript student commenting on the likeness of Paterson to another girl, whom he had encountered previously.

An elaborate account is also given by the pioneering surgeon Robert Liston in his personal diaries that describes a stand-up fight with Knox regarding the undignified treatment of Mary Paterson's body, but the story is largely unsubstantiated, so I have neglected it here as it adds little to the narrative.

In late 2010, following the publication of the first edition of this graphic novel, I came into contact with a New Jersey based history professor, Lisa Rosner, who was awaiting publication of her lengthily titled book *The Anatomy Murders, Being the True Story of Edinburgh's Notorious Burke and Hare and the Man of Science Who Abetted Them in the Commission of Their Most Heinous Crimes*. Rosner's book is one of the most thorough and professional I have encountered to date, expertly-researched, picking over the finer points of the case and providing forensic analysis of the available information. During her research, Rosner uncovered records from the Edinburgh Magdalene Asylum, and discovered revolving door in-patient entries starting in 1826 pertaining to a Mary Paterson.

Professor Rosner subsequently found a later discharge date of 8 April, 1828 - the day before Paterson's murder - but, while making no direct assertion that they are one and the same, presents a strong argument to dispel an notion that she was involved romantically with any of Knox's students.

CHAPTER EIGHT – In Cold Blood

PAGE 26

Burke continues his confession on this page, with comments concerning the Paterson murder (see previous appendix) and mentions the murder of a washer-woman in "September or October", then a woman named McDougal, who happened to be a relation of Helen McDougal, Burke's common-law wife. In all likelihood, the washer-woman was murdered in early September, and the McDougal woman in late September, although, I have no evidence to support this theory, other than my own speculative notion.

The murder of James Wilson probably took place in early or mid-October, since the final murder is known to have taken place on Friday 31 October. As touched upon here, and detailed in the next appendix, Burke ends page 26 with details surrounding the most publicised of the West Port murders: the allurement, murder and disposal of 'Daft' James Wilson.

CHAPTER NINE - For A Sheep As A Lamb

PAGES 27-32

Jamie Wilson was allegedly murdered by Burke and Hare at some stage between Sunday 5 and Sunday 26 October, 1828. The event probably contributed to the duo's downfall more than any of the other murders, with the exception of Mary Paterson and the final victim Mary Docherty. Following Burke's trial, the family of James Wilson attempted to bring private proceedings against Hare, but were dismissed on the grounds that he was immune from prosecution because of the unique agreement he had secured in return for testifying against Burke.

The events depicted in these pages are largely an invention, although some are taken from details given by both Hugh Douglas and Owen Dudley Edwards, among others. 'Daft' Jamie Wilson was allegedly a popular public figure in Edinburgh - akin to a village idiot - who purportedly entertained people in the streets with amusing anecdotes and songs in return for money and food. Much was written about the teenager after Burke's trial, largely in the form of poems, broadsides and songs; but I suspect his popularity developed *after* his death, not before it. Owen Dudley Edwards suggests that Burke and Hare must have known Daft Jamie prior his murder, since there was too much folklore circulating about the youngster's life for it to have originated in posthumous manufacture. I do not doubt that Burke or Hare may have been aware of the youth's existence, but I find it absurd that the stories about Jamie's life were too abundant to have been invented after his demise. The speculation that often accompanies the death of a local figure can often vary quite dramatically from person to person - especially when the circumstances are violent or suspicious. Stories of murder often grow in the telling, and fable soon replaces fact; particularly so in the case of Burke and Hare's antics. Edwards seems happy to assert that rumours about Burke and Hare's wives being involved in the murders were entirely an invention of the press, but does not apply the same logic in the case of Jamie Wilson. In truth, 'Daft' Jamie was probably never as popular at any time living, as he would be in death.

A case in point is the joke made by Jamie on page 27. In Hugh Douglas' *Burke & Hare: The True Story*, an account is given of the 'braces' anecdote, attributed to Jamie as part of a play by the Kinloch Players who toured Scotland until the 1950s - with Benjamin Disraeli and William Gladstone as the two principal subjects of the joke. However, Mr Pickering pointed out to me that both Disraeli and Gladstone were relatively unknown figures in 1828, and neither took up office as Prime Minister of Great Britain for 40 years, which indicates that the story was almost certainly manufactured long after Jamie's demise and without any notion towards historical accuracy.

I replaced the subjects of the story with Spencer Perceval and the Duke of Wellington, both of whom held the office of Prime Minister in Jamie's lifetime and would have been reasonably well-known to the general public. Additionally, braces were only invented in 1822, and were not in widespread use until the mid-19th Century, so the story is merely added here as an illustrative aside to introduce the ill-fated idiot Jamie Wilson and allow me the opportunity to emphasise the likelihood of Jamie's popularity being manufactured.

In his confession, Burke describes Hare as the principal actor in the murder of Jamie, but I have also included Hare's common-law wife in these scenes, as I strongly suspect she was influential in many of the murders, not just that of Jamie Wilson. Almost every biographer of the case concurs with this. Brian Lane, in *The Murder Book of Days* (Headline Books, 1995) cites Hare's common-law wife as Maggie Laird, while Owen Dudley Edwards first cites Laird as her maiden name, then later in his book, mentions that her first husband's name was James Logue (some of the official documents refer to her surname as 'Log'). According to Hugh Douglas, she was fairly well known as 'Lucky' Hare - which would eventually prove to be fitting, for although she was arrested and indicted with Burke, Hare and Burke's common-law wife Helen McDougal, she was released following the trial and is recorded in some journals as having spent her remaining days as a nanny in Paris. Her wise choice of following Hare in turning King's Evidence allowed her to escape justice also. As with Burke and Hare, 'Lucky' Hare was also Irish, while Helen McDougal, Burke's common-law wife, was the only Scot among the quartet.

The title of this chapter is taken from a quote in the Courant Confession, concerning the murder of James Wilson, which was singled out as "flowery" by Owen Dudley Edwards in *Burke & Hare*. The quote states: "Burke declares that Mrs Hare led poor Jamie in as a dumb lamb to the slaughter and a sheep to the shearers". Again, this suggests to me the desire of a specific individual to over-emphasise Jamie's death in order to further implicate Lucky Hare in the murder. The quote is given further suspicion later in the Courant Confession when Burke is quoted as saying: "No-one being present at the murders but [ourselves]; [they thought] they might as well be hanged for a sheep as a lamb". The similarities between the two statements are fairly obvious.

The Courant Confession also contains two other similar phrases which I feel are too coincidental to have occurred separately, or to have originated from the same person. On the occasion of Mary Paterson, the Courant Confession states that she had: "twopence halfpenny held fast in her hand", then on the occasion of the murder of a "Mrs Hostler" (whom I decided not to name in my account since no name was given in the Official Confession) the Courant states: "Mrs Hostler had ninepence halfpenny in her hand, which they scarcely could get out of it after she was dead, so firmly was it grasped".

Make up your own mind, but both sets of remarks have a faint whiff of suspicion about them.

CHAPTER TEN – The Butcher, The Thief and the Boy Who Bought the Beef

PAGES 33-40

The scenes depicted on these pages probably appear slightly confusing at first glance. In essence, three different timelines are depicted in a horizontal fashion across the pages: the top narrative covers components of Burke's trial, while the middle segment takes the reader back to the day *after* the final murder. The bottom set of panels on each page depicts the *build-up* to the murder of Mary Docherty, the duo's final victim. This chapter was inserted as an expansion to my original script, which omitted details of Burke's trial because of space restrictions in the original 48-page format set down by Caliber Comics in the mid-1990s.

The information presented in the top set of panels is taken directly from the court transcriptions and requires little in the way of explanation. The characters featured are, variously: The Lord Justice

Stuart Beel's concept art for William Hare

Clerk the Right Hon. David Boyle; Lord Pitmilly, Lord Meadowbank and Lord McKenzie. Also depicted are Archibald Alison, one of the advocates-depute interviewing William Noble, the barman from Rymer's tavern, Anne Black, one of Burke and Hare's neighbours in the lodging house where Mary Docherty was murdered being interviewed by Alexander Wood. Hugh Alston, one of Burke and Hare's neighbours, provides evidence to Mr Alison. James Gray, a party reveller from the lodging house on the night Docherty was murdered provides evidence to Robert Dundas, the advocate depute. Finally, Hare gives evidence to Henry Cockburn, the counsel for Helen McDougal.

The middle and bottom sets of panels are largely an invention, but are drawn from information given at Burke's trial and taken from the official trial transcripts when the police were called after a considerable commotion at a Halloween party at John Broggan's lodging house.

Burke's trial was something of a major event of the era. In essence, Burke and Hare were the world's first media serial killers, with tales of their deeds published in newspapers up and down the country on a daily basis. Indeed, the French artist Madame Marie Toussaud attended Burke's trial at Edinburgh Court in order to obtain a likeness of the man to put him on display at her famous London waxworks.

The title of the chapter is taken from a popular children's nursery rhyme that sprang forth from the terrible events of 1828.

Will Pickering's concept art for Robert Knox

CHAPTER ELEVEN – To The Last

PAGE 41

Burke concludes his confession by detailing the murder of Mary Docherty (or Mary Campbell, depending on which account you read), which was, as he states, the murder that finally convicted him at his trial on Wednesday 24 December, 1828.

Owen Dudley Edwards and Hugh Douglas make much of Burke's trial and its intricate legalities, but the dramatic effect is somewhat lessened in a book of this format. So, I have avoided any depiction of the events other than the scenes covered in pages 33-40.

As mentioned earlier, the jury took 50 minutes to reach their verdict of guilty for Burke, and 'not proven' for Helen McDougal.

Scotland has a unique legal system, in that, even though we are considered part of the sovereignty of the United Kingdom, because of a long-feared tradition and Scottish right, we are permitted to retain our own laws. One of these laws states that if a jury finds insufficient evidence upon which to convict the accused, they are permitted to return a peculiar verdict of 'not proven'. It's a controversial verdict not without its problems, even in the modern era. The not proven verdict has shown to be a favourable option when the evidence is generally circumstantial or inadequate to convince a jury of outright guilt. However, there are many cases in Scottish legal history where the 'not proven' verdict has been returned in circumstances where the evidence would appear to favour a conviction. The stigma associated with the verdict generally implies guilt. Sir Walter Scott referred to the not proven option as the "bastard verdict".

Burke's final remarks on this page are taken directly from the Official Confession, and need little explanation.

CHAPTER TWELVE - The Sleep of the Just

PAGE 42

The sequence of events depicted here are best explained in the appendix to page 16 and 17.

CHAPTER THIRTEEN - The Last Of Mister Burke

PAGES 43-48

The events on these pages are taken from Owen Dudley Edwards' *Burke & Hare*.

According to most biographers, up to 25,000 people attended Burke's execution at Liberton's Wynd in Edinburgh at 8.15am on Wednesday 28 January, 1829. The city's wealthy elite – including Sir Walter Scott - lined the windows of the overlooking buildings, and the poor filled the streets in their masses. It is widely believed to be one of the largest assembled crowds in Edinburgh's history, the recent annual Hogmanay celebrations notwithstanding. The images depicted of Burke's hanging by Mr Pickering are drawn variously from images, including Thomas

Ireland's engraving of the execution can be found on the web, and was crucial reference for the spatial relationships between the High Kirk, County Hall, Liberton Wynd and the gallows platform. The rest of the street is reconstructed from innumerable paintings and photographs of individual buildings as far down Edinburgh's Royal Mile as John Knox's House, seen from an angle which could not have been achieved until Short's Observatory (now the Camera Obscura) opened in the 1850s.

Burke is depicted as slightly thinner than in previous encounters in these scenes – largely as a result of being fed only bread and water since his conviction. Will and I debated making him appear bald in these scenes, since several accounts claim it was tradition to shave the head of a condemned man before execution. Certainly, Burke's death mask depicts a completely bald pate, which would seem to reconcile with this. However, while we have been able to establish that the head of executed prisoners was often shaved post-mortem for the purposes of death masks, the only accounts we could find of pre-execution head shaving relates to recipients of the electric chair, where the removal of hair is part of the actual process. Ned Kelly and William Corder were both shaved after death, specifically for the purposes of mask-making. So, the images of Burke on these pages are based on an illustration of Burke that was allegedly drawn on the day of his execution.

Burke makes a muffled comment as the rope is being fastened around his neck on page 46 about the knot being "behind", which is recounted in almost every biography I have found on the subject of the West Port murders. The only conclusion reached is that the knot should have been placed in front, where it is intended to choke the victim, but for some unknown reason was not. Judicial hangings prior to 1850 were carried out using the 'short drop' method, where the condemned dies of strangulation. Given the widespread ill-feeling towards the man, it is entirely possible that the misplacement of the knot was deliberate on the part of the hangman at Burke's execution, which would have undoubtedly resulted in his death being excessively and inhumanely prolonged. As depicted on these pages, Burke's executioner is depicted in normal clothing – and not the traditional 'black mask' of movie lore – as we were unable to locate any evidence to direct us otherwise. Several accounts of Burke's death cite a lengthy process of his struggling and kicking, which reconciles with the notion that he suffocated, as opposed to his vertebrae being severed instantly.

Edinburgh's streets as depicted by Will Pickering

Following his demise, Burke's body was handed over to the medical faculty at Edinburgh University as decreed by the Lord Justice Clerk the Right Hon. David Boyle at his sentencing, where it was publicly dissected by Dr Robert Knox's closest rival, Professor Alexander Monro. Back on page four, readers will note Burke mentioning that on the first visit to Surgeons' Square, Hare had originally been looking for one of "Doctor Monro's men", but were guided instead to 10 Surgeons' Square by "a person like a student" – in this case, a young Charles Darwin. It seems ironic that through a chance encounter, a strange twist of fate evolved, and perhaps had Burke and Hare been directed instead to Monro's halls, Knox would have been the likely recipient of Burke's body after the hanging. And, perhaps Knox would not have entered into the whole sordid mess in the first place.

Burke's dissected body was viewed by more than

30,000 people, and a riot between students and the police erupted outside the lecture hall as crowds jostled to catch a glimpse of the corpse. Many people paid a fee to pass through the room where the dissection lecture had taken place, and pieces of Burke's skin, along with the gallows and rope that hanged him were sold as souvenirs afterwards. A notebook, allegedly bound in his skin, remains on display in Surgeons' Hall in Edinburgh, although its authenticity is unverified.

Burke's bones also remain on display in at Edinburgh University, which I personally find morbidly fascinating. Professor Matthew Kaufman, at the Anatomy Department in Edinburgh University's Medical School, allowed myself and the original artist of Burke and Hare, Stuart Beel, access to the private museum to view Burke's skeleton in 1997. Upon my return in January 2009 (coincidentally, on the 180th anniversary of the eve of Burke's hanging), Dr Gordon Findlater was kind enough to guide myself and Will around the museum and enlighten us to some additional facts about the Burke and Hare case.

The cabinet in which Burke's skeleton is displayed has the added bonus of containing life masks of both murderers, along with Burke's death mask – which was cast after his hanging. It was a chilling thrill to gaze upon the faces of two of the most notorious men in Scottish criminal history; so special credit and thanks are due to Professor Kaufman and Dr Findlater for their kind hospitality on both occasions.

The poem recited by Burke on page 43 was written by the Scottish national poet Robert Burns and is entitled *Man Was Made To Mourn*. Born in 1759, Burns developed an early affection for literature, and, between 1784 and 1788, whilst working as a farm labourer, he produced much of his best and most celebrated poetry. He died in 1796, aged just 37. Today, he is held by many to be among the greatest poets of all time.

Burke's request for a handkerchief - upon which the poem and a likeness of Burns was stitched - is also taken from Owen Dudley Edwards' *Burke & Hare*.

CHAPTER FOURTEEN - The Last Of Mister Black

PAGE 49

The scene depicted here is based on events given by Hugh Douglas, Owen Dudley Edwards and numerous other biographers. As agreed by law, William Hare was released as 'Mister Black' on Thursday 5 February, 1829 to a mail coach at Newington, where he was taken south to its first stop at Noblehouse. He was recognised by one of his fellow-passengers, Douglas Sandford, the lawyer who had represented the family of Jamie Wilson in court during their failed attempt to bring private proceedings against Hare. Further down the mainland at Dumfries, Hare's identity was made known to the local inhabitants and a crowd of about 8,000 people gathered to catch sight of his arrival. After a tense struggle, police intervention ensured that Hare was led safely from a local inn and put on a coach bound for Annan.

Hare was last seen heading South, at Carlisle, on Saturday 7 February. His possible whereabouts thereafter are shrouded in mystery, but will be briefly discussed towards the end of these notes.

CHAPTER FIFTEEN - The Clearing

PAGES 50-53

The scene on these pages depicts a conversation between Robert Knox and his friend, Dr Robert Adams. It is based on information given by Knox's former student and biographer William Roughead. The "Robert Christison" mentioned in the dialogue was a rival anatomist of Knox who was appointed to conduct an enquiry into the 'body-purchasing' scandal. However, the committee hearing took place in advance of the date given on page 50.

Christison was professor of medical jurisprudence at Edinburgh University and had direct involvement in the trial of William Burke, providing much deliberation from the witness box over the questionable possibility of the final victim's death having been caused by violence. The somewhat suggestive dialogue between Knox and Adams concerning Burke's impending confession is purely fiction and I have no grounds upon which to base the scathing accusation that a conspiracy took place over the production of the Courant Confession, despite anything I have said previously about its authenticity. However, it does follow that Christison would have been keen to avoid any scrutiny, since further investigation could have opened up a whole new can of worms for the entire Edinburgh medical establishment.

The scene depicted with the little girl is as presented in Henry Lonsdale's account of Knox's life.

CHAPTER SIXTEEN - Letters and Lies

PAGE 54

It goes without saying that this scene is entirely fictitious. No evidence, other than my own fanciful notion, exists to suggest that Knox sent any such letter or bribe to the Procurator Fiscal in order that an amended version of Burke's confession could be published in the Edinburgh Evening Courant.

However, Brian Bailey alludes to a complex series of conspiracies regarding pamphlets and confessions that were produced in various Edinburgh publications following Burke's execution, none of which are supportable by any substantial fact.

The only pronouncement Knox made regarding the entire affair was in a letter to the *Caledonian Mercury* on 17 March, 1829 where he defended his position and praised the findings of the committee, while criticising their decision to chastise him for not taking more care over where he procured cadavers from.

CHAPTER SEVENTEEN - Who Will Venture To Pronounce?
PAGES 55-56

The scene on this page depicts the writer and poet Sir Walter Scott commenting on a letter received from David Paterson, an assistant of Dr Robert Knox, who provided evidence at Burke's trial. Paterson's letter offered to provide Scott with interesting anecdotes about Knox's dealings with Burke and Hare. However, the notion that Scott would write about the murders was received poorly and much of the dialogue in these scenes is taken from letters and journals compiled by Scott himself. The individual chatting with Scott in these scenes is Sir George Sinclair, who visited the author on 23 January, 1829 with the intention of inviting him to participate on the committee investigating Knox's alleged involvement in the murders. Scott was incensed at the suggestion and declined the committee's offer, as detailed in his various letters and referenced by Brian Bailey, among others. The letter sent by Paterson was commented on in Scott's journal in April, but I have combined Scott's reactions to both communiqués as taking place on the same day for fictional purposes.

Sir Walter Scott was a prolific Scottish historical novelist and poet popular throughout Europe during the early 19th Century. He lived at 6 Shandwick Place, as depicted by Will on these pages. He is also listed in various publications as having lived at 39 North Castle Street, but had sold the property in 1826, before spending time in various properties around the country until construction on his stately home of Abbotsford in the Scottish Borders was completed. Scott is widely considered to be the originator of the historical novel, and wrote the book upon which the movie *Rob Roy* was based, among other classic works such as *Ivanhoe*, *Waverley* and *Heart of Midlothian*.

Monuments to Scott's memory adorn the city centres of both Glasgow and Edinburgh and are among the largest free-standing memorials in Scotland. His image also adorns every denomination of bank note issued by the Bank of Scotland, the country's oldest banking establishment. As a writer, he was internationally famous in his own lifetime and his work influenced Charles Dickens, William Makepeace Thackeray and Robert Louis Stevenson (who did write about the West Port Murders). Scott also attended Burke's trial, and the subsequent hanging at Liberton's Wynd - and inspected the lodging house at 10 Tanner's Close as part of his involvement in the case.

He retired to Abbotsford, where he died in 1832.

CHAPTER EIGHTEEN – Onwards To Glasgow

PAGE 57

The fictitious scene on this page summarises Knox's departure to Glasgow, having been struck off the medical register and turned down for the role as Chair of Pathology and Physiology at the University of Edinburgh. In Glasgow, he worked for a time at the Argyle Square Medical School, with varying accounts citing him as leaving for London in 1842, following the death of his wife and one of his children. Knox never reached the heights of fame in his field that he was destined for and spent the rest of his life touring the country giving lectures before settling in London, where he worked at the Brompton Hospital for Consumption and Diseases of the Chest (more on which, later).

The house at Newington Place, depicted in the first panel, is a fine example of the intense research carried out by Mr Pickering in the course of illustrating my script. According to Will, by the time Newington Place appears on the 1843 Ordnance Survey map, it is clearly recognisable as the terrace of townhouses still there today, half-hidden behind a row of shops and re-designated as 1-17 Newington Road (odd numbers only: the OS map shows it as 1-9 running in the opposite direction). Robert Knox lived at 4 Newington Place in 1829, as confirmed by contemporary reports of the angry mob that besieged his house in the aftermath of the Burke trial to burn an effigy of the man in protest at his alleged involvement in the crimes; but was it the same house that was there 15 years later, or an earlier building in the same general vicinity?

To find out, Will had to go further back in his research. West Newington House, just across the road, was built in 1805 as part of a development scheme initiated by the then landowner, the surgeon Benjamin Bell (the grandfather of Joseph Bell, whose observational and deductive skills famously inspired Sir Arthur Conan Doyle to create the famous detective Sherlock Holmes), but progress in the vicinity seems to have been reasonably slow: *Thomson's Atlas of Scotland* for 1820 shows no structures on the Newington Place plot, and a feu map as late as 1826 shows only an empty field assigned to a 'Mr Reid'. Arniston Place, the next block south, appears on both maps, which suggests that it was not merely an oversight by a lazy cartographer. The conclusion Will reached was that the current 11 Newington Road, behind the New China Town Cantonese restaurant currently situated on the street, is indeed the former home of Robert Knox, who probably purchased it as a suburban new-build sometime in 1826-1828. As Will commented, it was a relief to finally figure it out, and one of the nice things about Georgian architecture relates to its mathematical regularity; the original design can easily be extrapolated from even a partial view.

The arrangement of Knox's study as depicted in this scene is entirely Will Pickering's invention, although several of his knicknacks are taken from the display about his life at Surgeons' Hall in Edinburgh.

CHAPTER NINETEEN - Of Winters Yet To Come

PAGES 58-59

The scene depicted here, whilst somewhat tenuous, has grounds in remote possibility. We have presented a fictitious meeting at the Brompton Hospital for Consumption and Diseases of the Chest between Robert Knox and his former student William Fergusson - who went on to become Sergeant-Surgeon to Queen Victoria and was created a baronet in 1866 – and a young Sir William Withey Gull.

According to Stephen Knight in *Jack the Ripper: The Final Solution* (George G. Harrap & Co Ltd, London), William Gull may (or may not) have been responsible for the 'Jack the Ripper' murders in Whitechapel, London in 1888. William Withey Gull was born in 1816, the son of a barge owner and the youngest of eight children. In 1837, Benjamin Harrison, treasurer of Guy's Hospital took him to London and employed him there. In 1843 he was made a lecturer in the hospital's medical school, before becoming an assistant physician in 1851. In 1856 he became full physician and was made a fellow of the Royal Society in 1869. Queen Victoria created him a baronet in 1872 in recognition of the care he had shown in attending the Prince of Wales during an attack of typhoid fever in 1871. My reasons for inserting the scene are thus: Gull would have been aged 12 at the time of the West Port murders, undoubtedly developing an interest in medical science and almost certainly aware of Burke and Hare's deeds in Edinburgh. In 1856, aged 39, he had embarked on an advanced stage of his medical career. It is entirely feasible that he associated with individuals such as Fergusson and it is equally possible that he would have attended various hospitals in London in order that a wide experience of medical practice could be obtained. Even if he did not actually keep company with Fergusson, it would seem likely that the two at least knew, or had heard of each other, given their elevated social status as Royal physicians. However, *Gull and Knox* ever meeting is somewhat unlikely, especially under such circumstances, but it is possible, given the narrow focus of their respective medical fields and their geographical proximity. My only other reason for inserting this scene is for the fun of it, especially given the similarities between the two cases and the coincidences involved. The Anatomy Act spoken of at the bottom of page 37 was a law enacted in 1832, dealing specifically with the problem of bodysnatching (with specific reference to the West Port murders, although not entirely attributed to the tragedy). It implemented new legislation permitting surgeons to receive bodies donated by the public for the advancement of medical science and changed medicine as we know it today.

EPILOGUE - A Final Exchange

PAGE 60

The final scene on this page is also fiction, although is based on evidence given by J B Atlay in his *Famous Trials of the Century* (London, 1899). Despite the lack of physical evidence to determine William Hare's final whereabouts (or his origin, for that matter), Atlay asserted that many Londoners would recollect from their childhood the principal attraction on Oxford Street in London being that of an old blind-beggar "who, with dog and stick was wont to solicit alms from passers-by. His story was on the lips of every nursemaid, and he was pointed out to awe-struck children as being William Hare, one of the actors in the West Port murders."

As mentioned previously, Robert Knox eventually moved to London in 1842, following the death of his wife, where he spent the remaining years of his life working in the Brompton Hospital for Consumption and Diseases of the Chest from 1856 onwards, writing about his medical work and producing a book about fishing, of all things. Numerous biographers state that Knox worked in the Brompton Cancer Hospital. However, during his research, Will discovered that the building and its facilities were later taken over by the Royal Marsden, but the two were still separate institutions when Knox worked at the Brompton. Knox eventually died in Fulham, on 20 December 1862, and was buried at Brookwood Cemetery near Woking, Surrey. Despite any alleged involvement in the West Port murders, his punishment lasted for the rest of his life in every sense. The depicted meeting between Hare (sans dog) and Knox is purely for dramatical purposes, and in all likelihood did not take place. However, I think it is an interesting notion to suggest that perhaps money changed hands between the doctor and the Devil one last time…

Martin Conaghan
Glasgow, August 2009
(Updated September 2011).

BIBLIOGRAPHY

Burke and Hare: The True Story. Hugh Douglas (Robert Hale and Co. 1973).

Burke & Hare. Owen Dudley Edwards (Polygon 1980).

Burke and Hare: The Year of The Ghouls. Brian Bailey (Mainstream 2002).

Burke and Hare. William Roughead (Edinburgh and London: W. Hodge & Company, Ltd., 1921).

Burke & Hare Crime Archive. Alanna Knight (National Archives 2007).

The Life of Dr. Knox. C. Carter Blake 1871.

The Murder Book of Days. Brian Lane (Headline Books, 1995).

A Sketch of the Life and Writings of Robert Knox the Anatomist. Henry Lonsdale (London: Macmillan, 1870).

Fiendish Killers. Anne Williams et al (Futura Books 2007).

The Body-Snatcher. Robert Louis Stevenson (Pall Mall Christmas Extra #13 Dec 1884).

Historic South Edinburgh. Charles J. Smith. (Charles Skilton Ltd, 1978).

Means To A Kill - An Encyclopaedia of Murder. Jon E. Lewis, (Headline Books, 1994).

The Canongate Burns: The Complete Poems and Songs of Robert Burns, ed. Andrew Noble and Patrick Scott Hogg (2001; Edinburgh: Canongate, 2003).

Famous Trials of the Century. J B Atlay (London, 1899).

Jack the Ripper: The Final Solution. Stephen Knight (George G. Harrap & Co Ltd, London).

From Hell. Alan Moore and Eddie Campbell (Top Shelf Comics).

West Port Murders (Thos Ireland 1829).

Modern Athens. T H Shepherd (Jones & Co 1829).

Metropolitan Improvements. (Jones & Co 1827).

Old and New Edinburgh. James Grant (Cassells 1876).

Edinburgh As It Was. C S Minto (Hendon 1974).

A History of Lothian and Borders Police. T W Archibald (ltd. ed. 1990)

British History Online: www.british-history.ac.uk

Journal. Sir Walter Scott (Oliver & Boyd 1950).

Edinburgh Evening Courant, edition: 7 February 1829.

Caledonian Mercury, edition: 17 March 1829.

The Body-Snatcher (1945). Robert Wise (director).

The Doctor and the Devils. Dylan Thomas (screenplay), Freddie Francis (director) (1985).

The Horrors of Burke and Hare. Ernle Bradford (screenplay), Vernon Sewell (director) (1972).

The Flesh and the Fiends. (1960). John Gilling (writer/director).

The Anatomist (TV play 1980). Pharic MacLaren (producer), James Bridie (playwright)

BBC Living Legends documentary presented by Magnus Magnusson.

Burke and Hare: The Musical. (1996). Stephen Murphy (director).

The Anatomy Murders, Being the True Story of Edinburgh's Notorious Burke and Hare and the Man of Science Who Abetted Them in the Commission of Their Most Heinous Crimes. Lisa Rosner (University of Pennsylvania Press 2010).

BONUS GALLERY

Featuring the work of (in order):

Dave Hill
Nulsh
Alex Ronald
Lynsey Hutchinson
Dave Alexander
Stuart Beel and PJ Holden
Stephen Daly
Stref
Hugh Parker
Gary Erskine
Frank Quitely

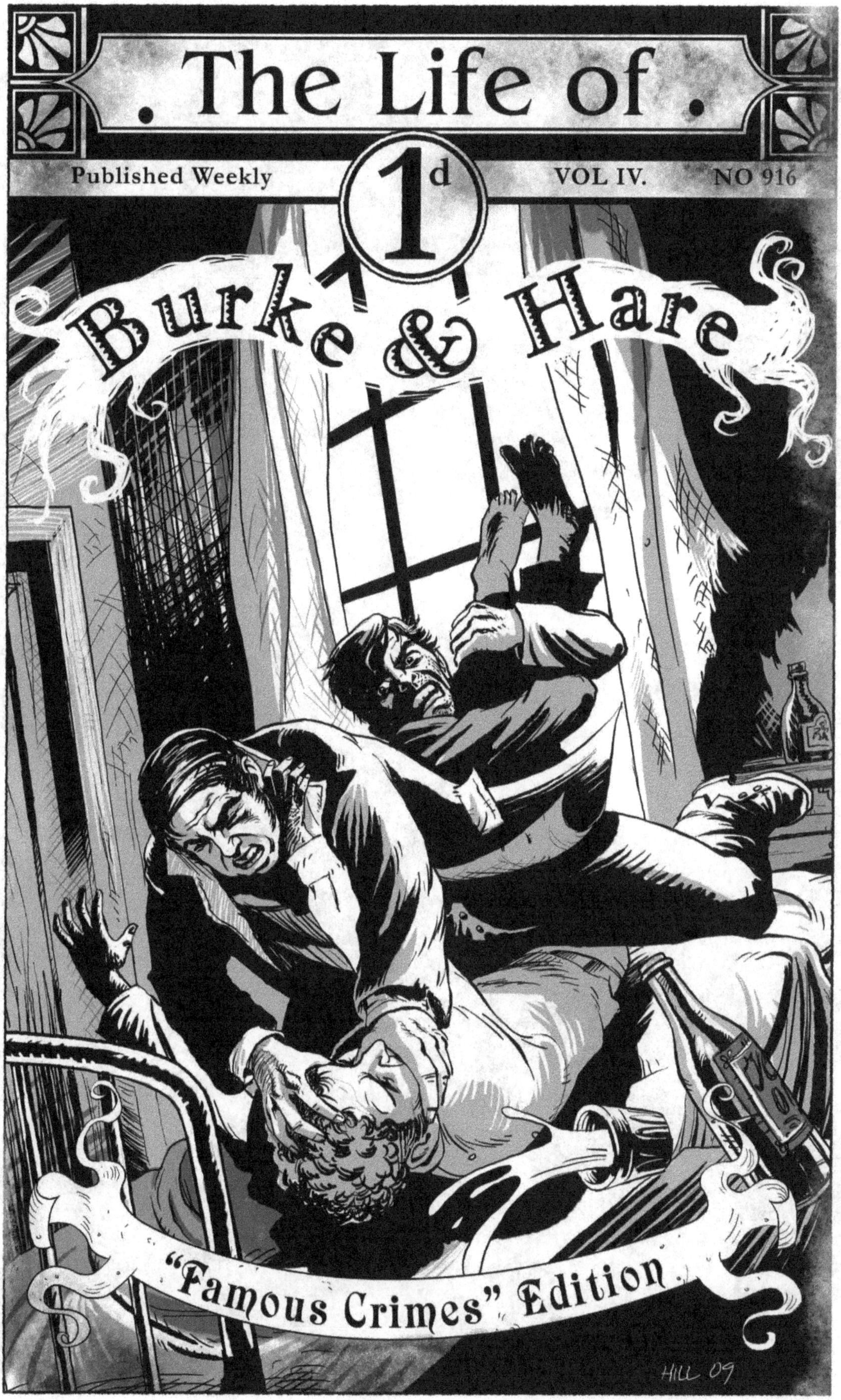

. The Life of .
Published Weekly
1d
VOL IV.
NO 916
Burke & Hare
"Famous Crimes" Edition
HILL 09

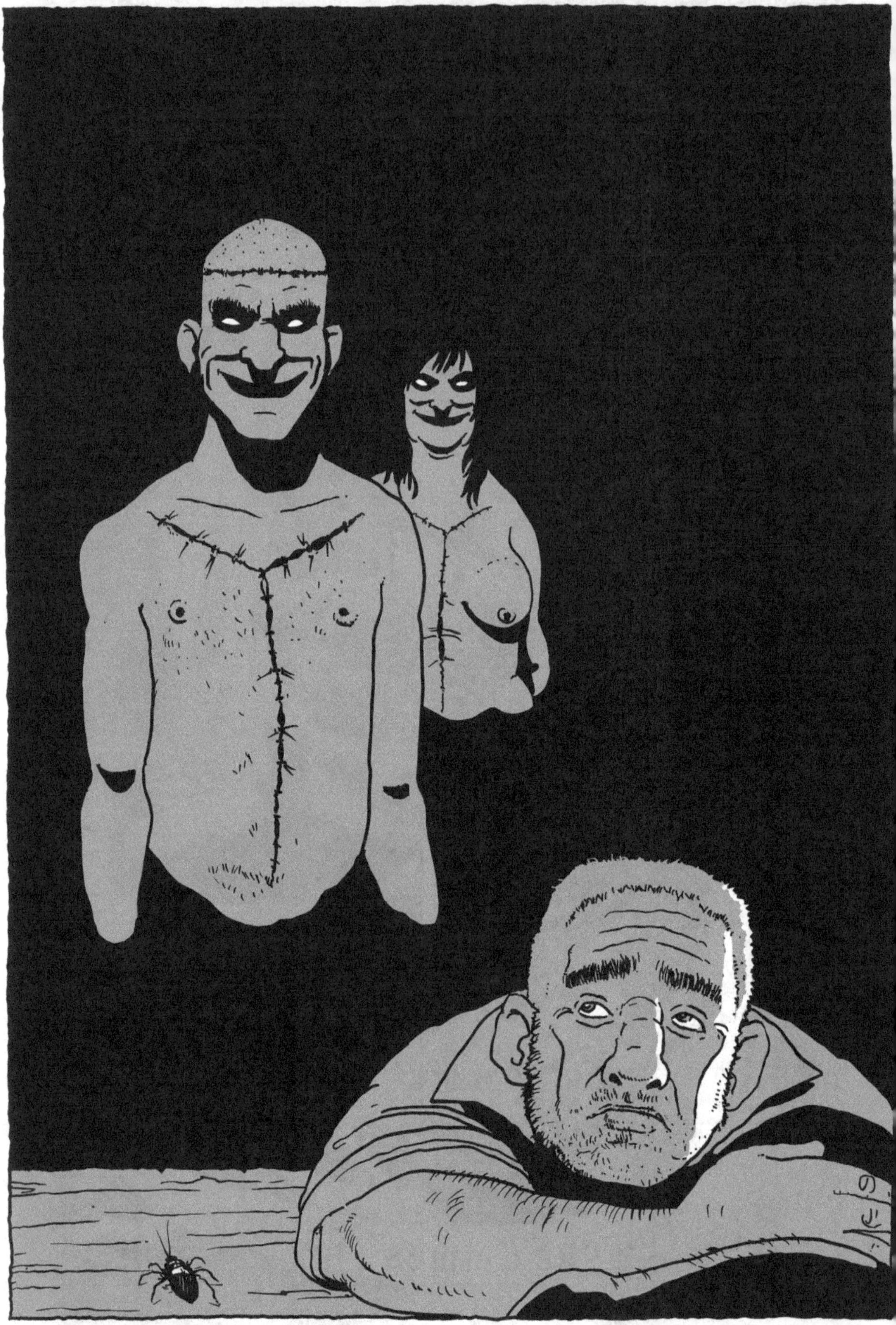

MURDER
PENNY Library

Vol IX — PUBLISHED WEEKLY BY CONAGHAN PRESS
NO 36 ROSE STREET, EDINBURGH — No. 22

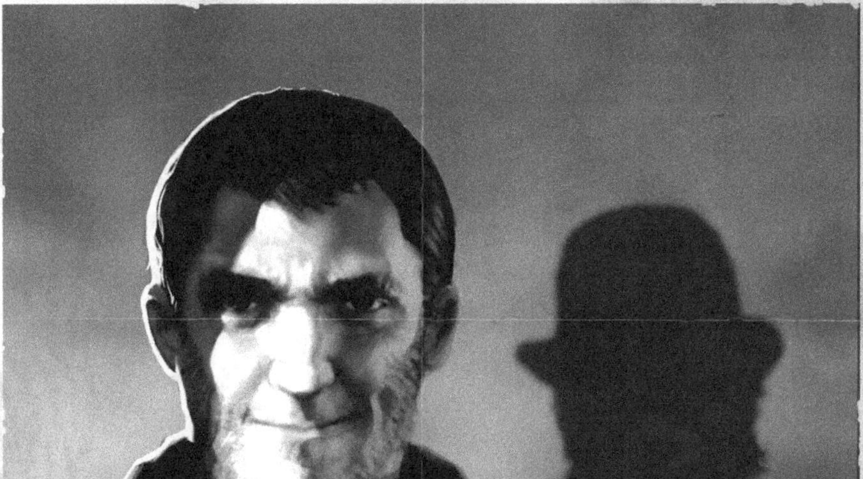
Lex

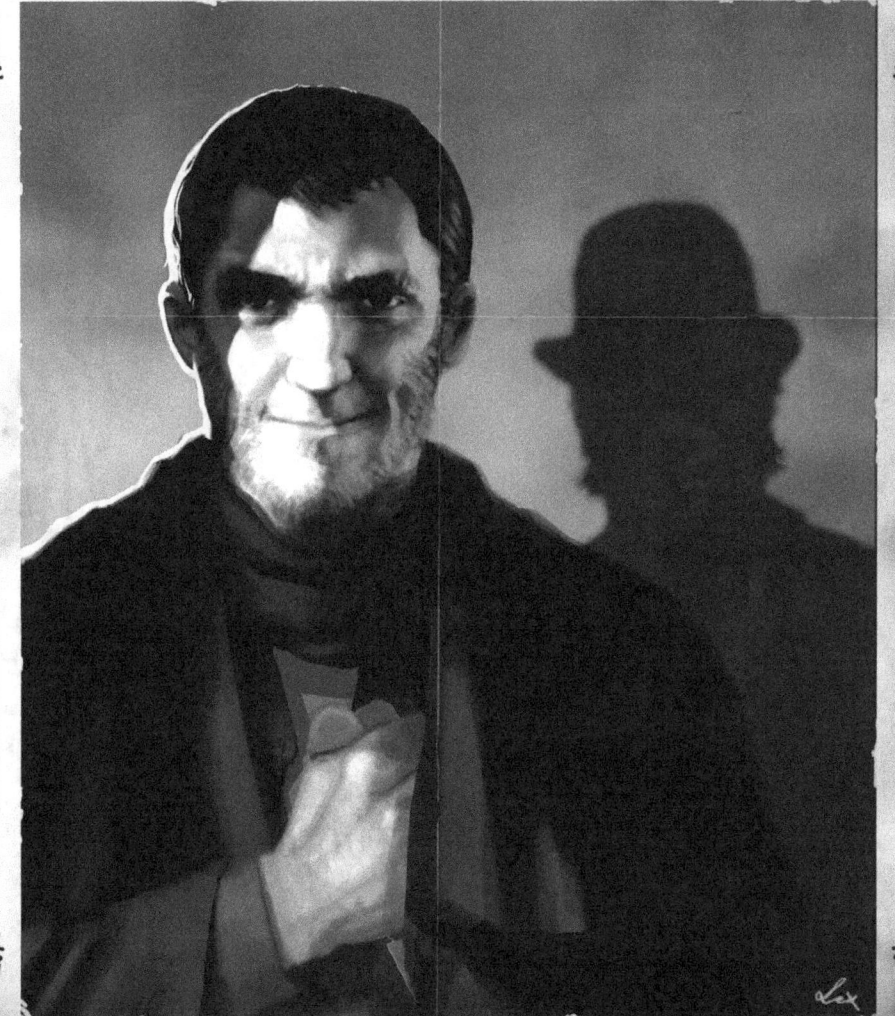

PRINTED IN GLASGOW

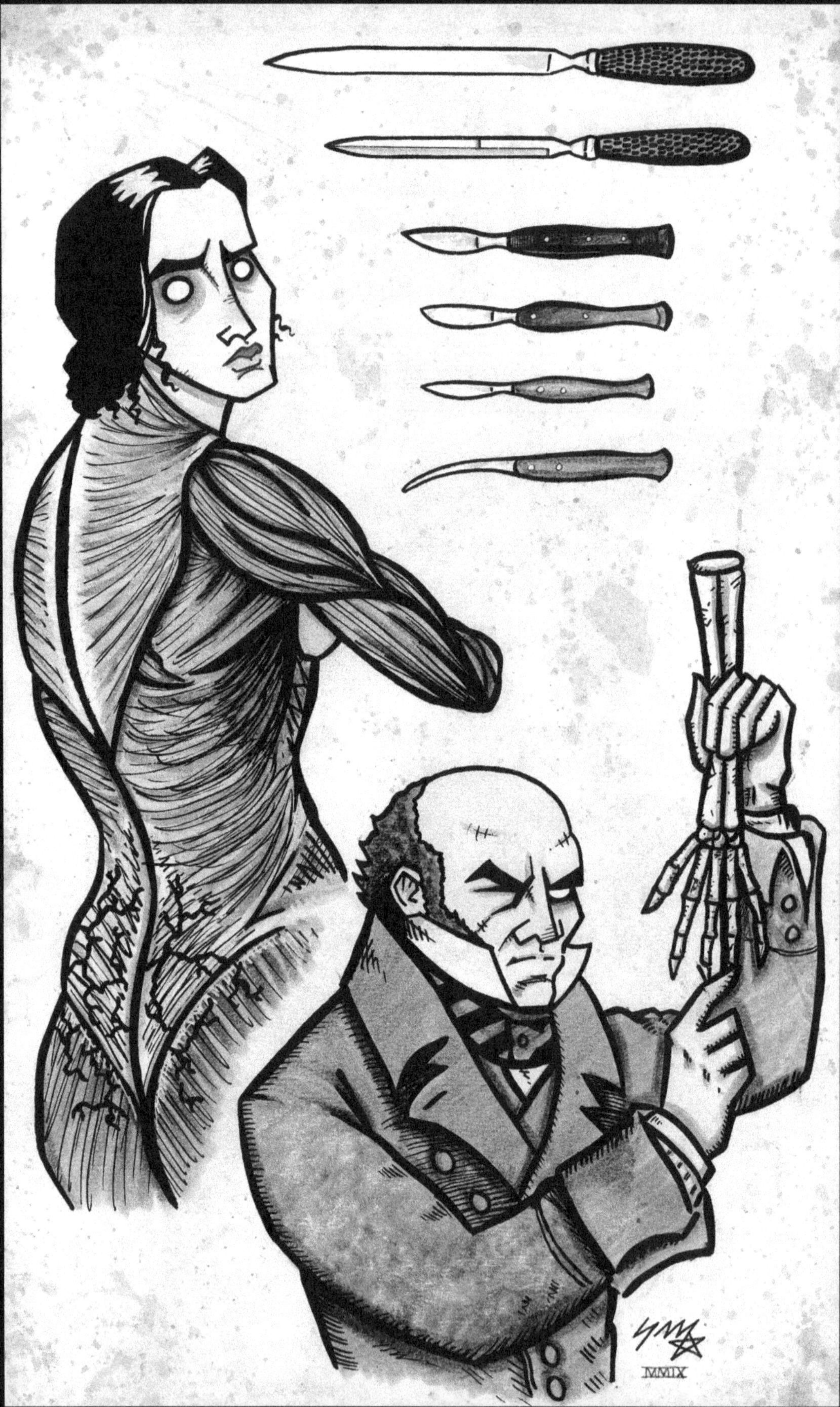
MMIX

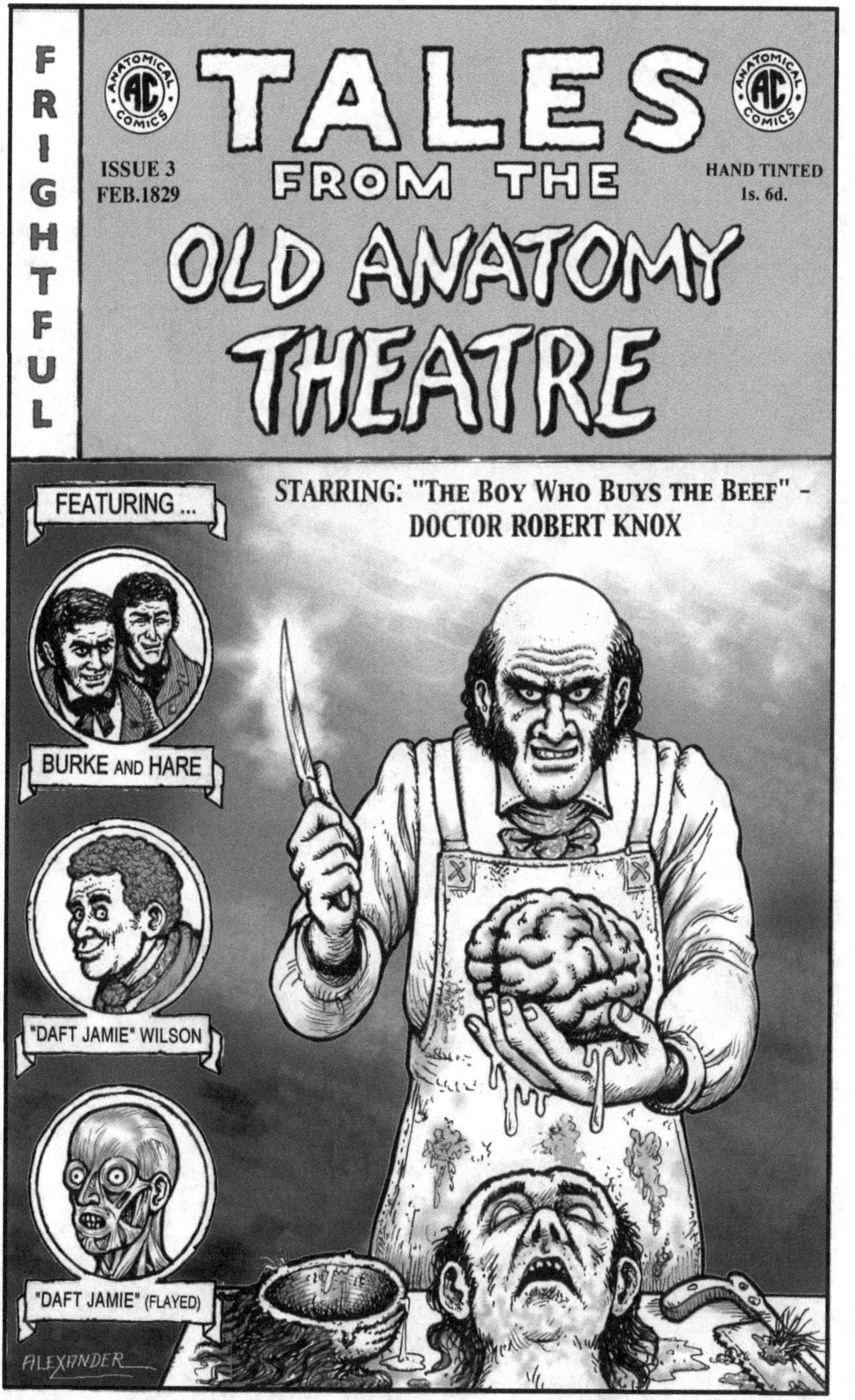
FRIGHTFUL
ANATOMICAL AC COMICS
TALES FROM THE OLD ANATOMY THEATRE
ANATOMICAL AC COMICS
ISSUE 3
FEB.1829
HAND TINTED
1s. 6d.
FEATURING ...
STARRING: "THE BOY WHO BUYS THE BEEF" -
DOCTOR ROBERT KNOX
BURKE AND HARE
"DAFT JAMIE" WILSON
"DAFT JAMIE" (FLAYED)
ALEXANDER

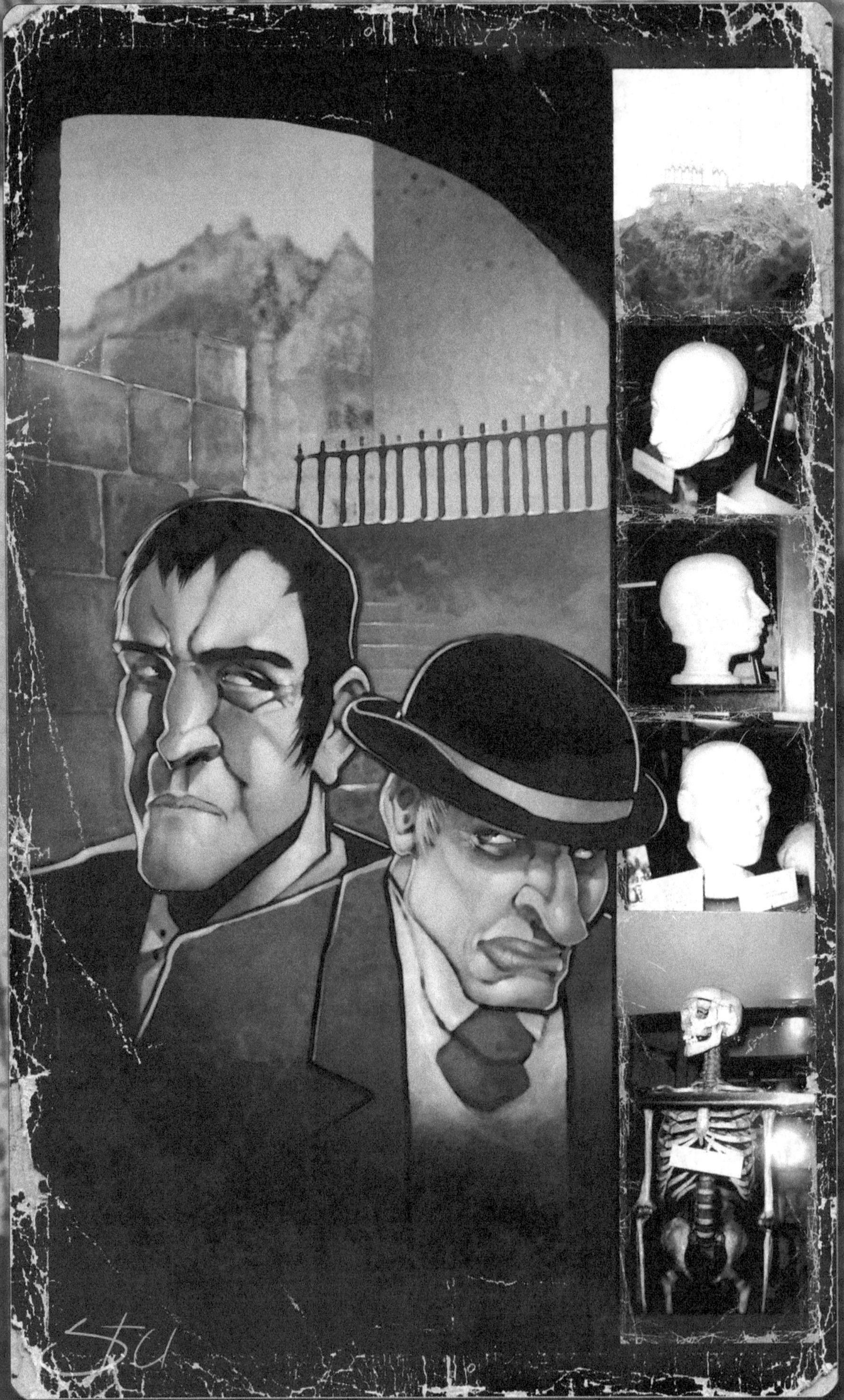

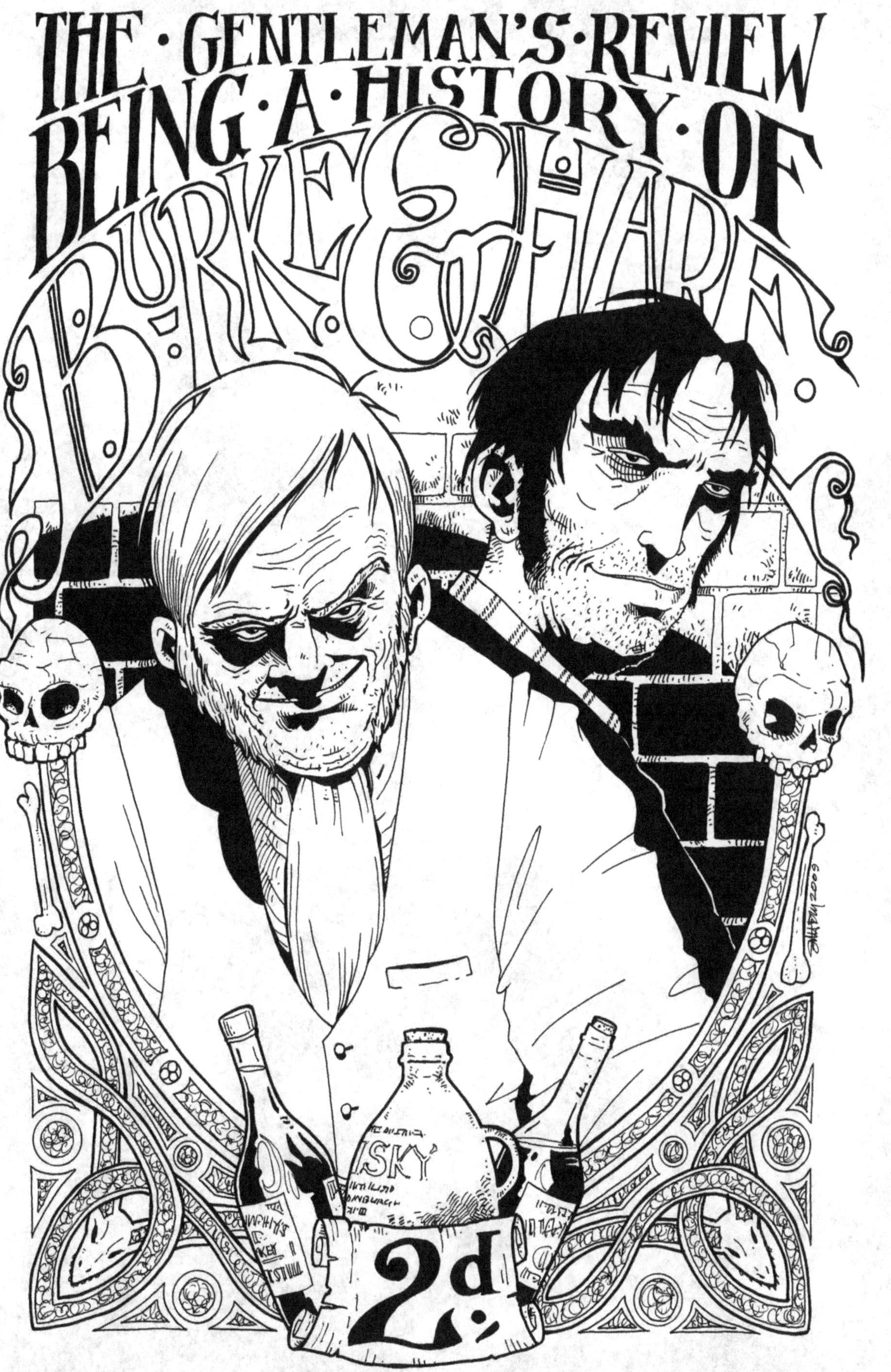
THE · GENTLEMAN'S · REVIEW
BEING · A · HISTORY · OF
BURKE & HARE
2d

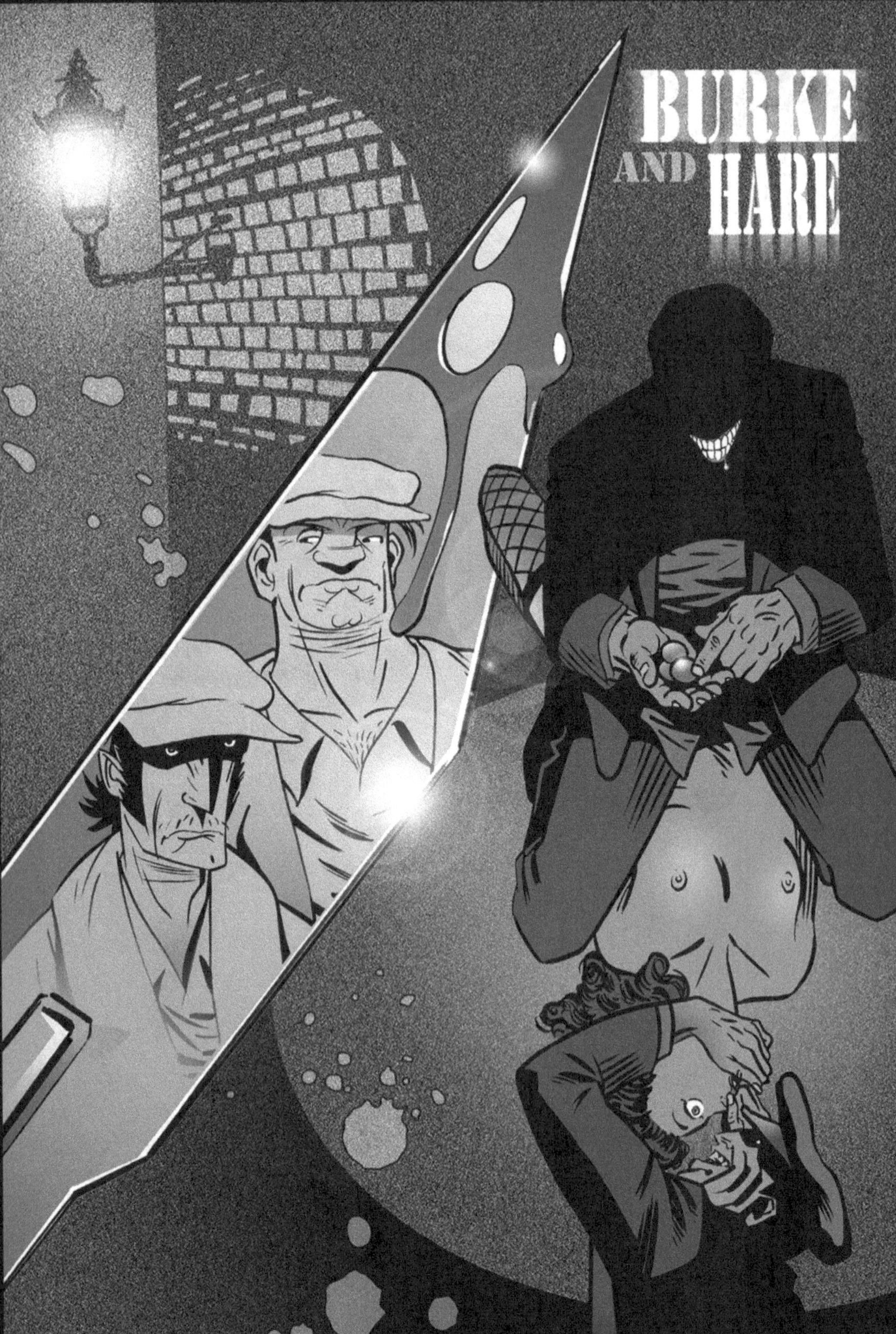
BURKE
AND HARE
STREF'

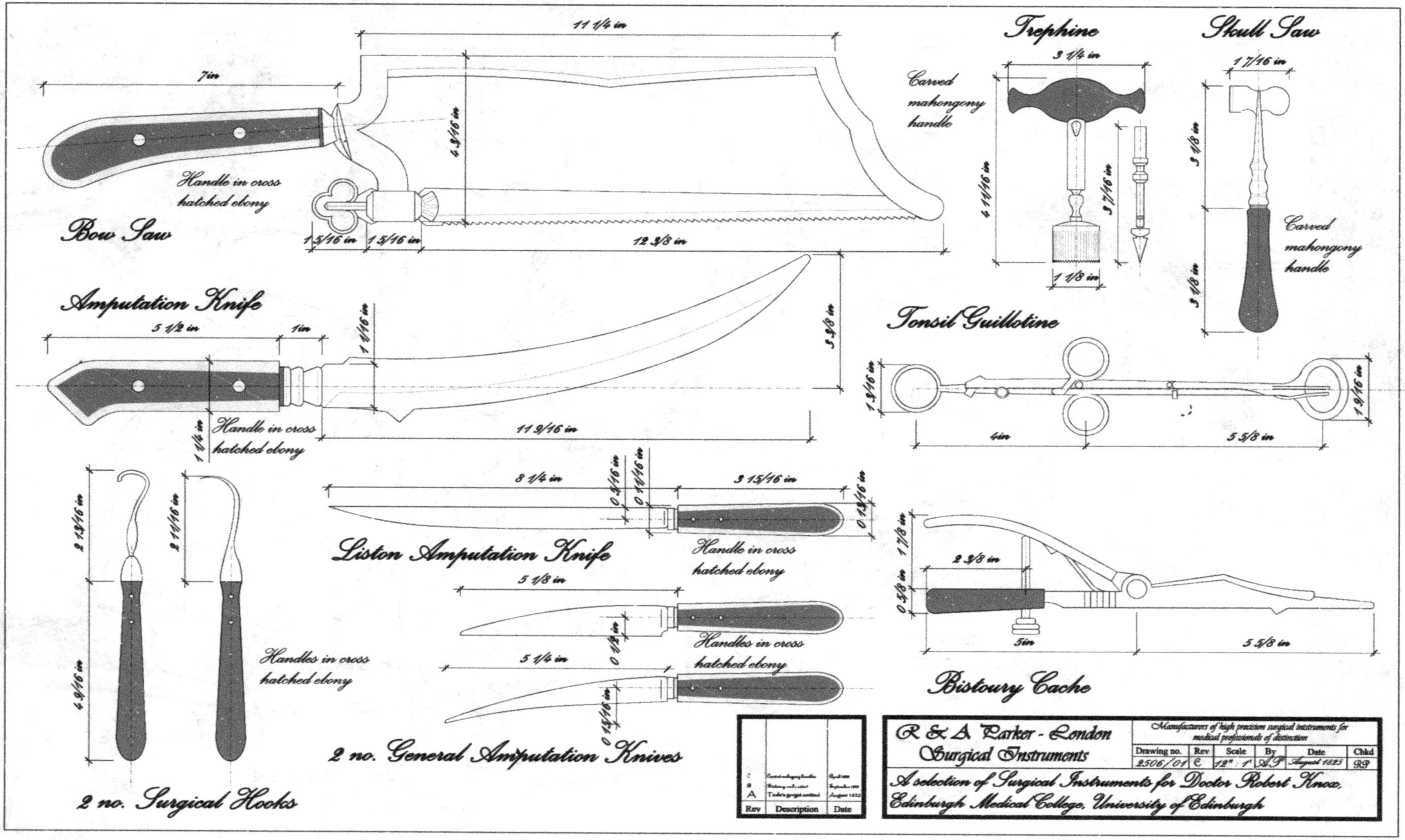
Bow Saw
Handle in cross hatched ebony
7in
11 1/4 in
12 3/8 in
Amputation Knife
Handle in cross hatched ebony
5 1/2 in
1in
11 9/16 in
Trephine
Carved mahongony handle
3 1/4 in
4 11/16 in
3 7/16 in
1 1/8 in
Skull Saw
Carved mahongony handle
1 7/16 in
3 1/8 in
Tonsil Guillotine
4in
5 5/8 in
Liston Amputation Knife
Handle in cross hatched ebony
8 1/4 in
3 15/16 in
2 no. General Amputation Knives
Handles in cross hatched ebony
5 1/8 in
5 1/4 in
2 no. Surgical Hooks
Handles in cross hatched ebony
Bistoury Cache
2 3/8 in
5in
5 5/8 in
R & A Parker - London
Surgical Instruments
Manufacturers of high precision surgical instruments for medical professionals of distinction
Drawing no. | Rev | Scale | By | Date | Chkd
2506/01 | C | 12" : 1' | AP | August 1825 | RP
A selection of Surgical Instruments for Doctor Robert Knox,
Edinburgh Medical College, University of Edinburgh
Rev | Description | Date

Remember me...

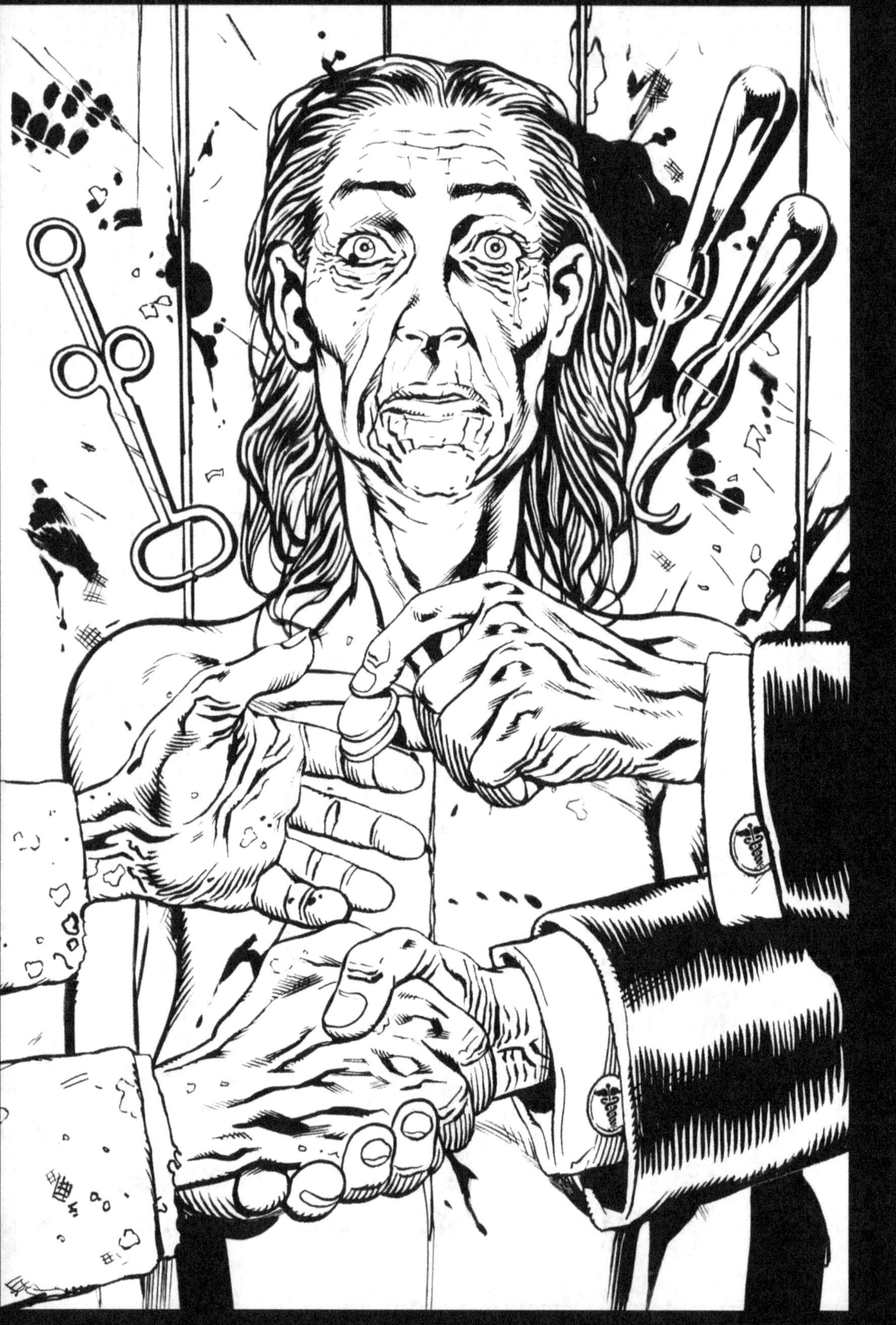

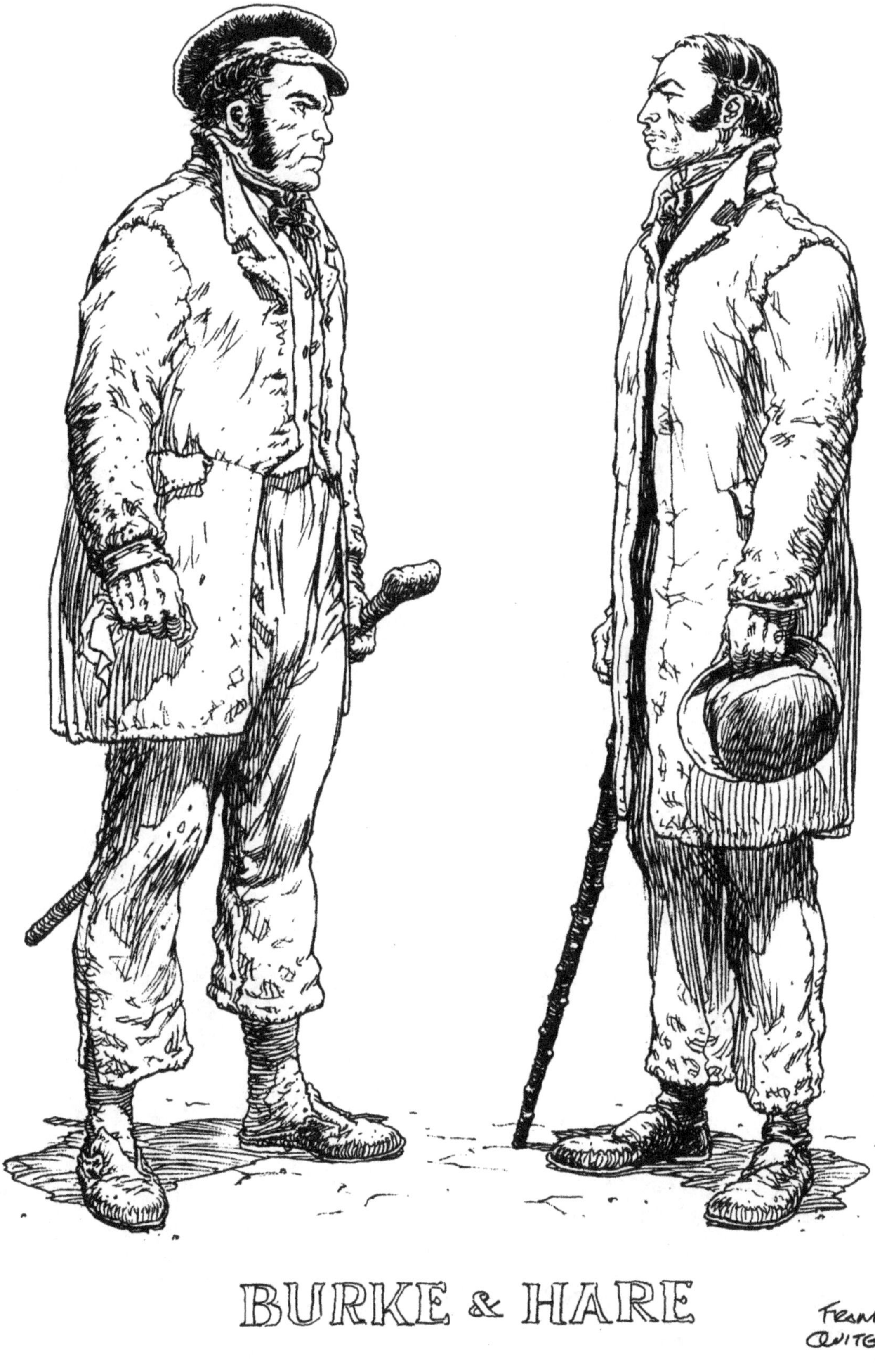

BURKE & HARE

FRANK QUITELY

GALLERY ARTIST BIOGRAPHIES

Dave Hill graduated from Glasgow School of Art and began his career as a painter with exhibitions in Glasgow, Edinburgh, Liverpool, and London. He has illustrated comic-books, video game characters and environment concepts, film and television storyboards, and children's books. Dave creates most of his work digitally, although he still dabbles in traditional media and paints in oils and watercolour.

Nulsh (real name Neil Hood) is an illustrator, cartoonist, and occasional animator - or as he puts it "likes to draw pictures and make up stories". His work has appeared in books, magazines, television, and self-published comics. He lives in Glasgow and his website is: www.nulsh.com

Alex Ronald has been an illustrator for 15 years. He started his career in the small press comics scene and progressed to top titles *Judge Dredd* and *Lobo* by the mid 90s. A change in direction led him to start developing 3D character and environment models for some of Scotland's top TV and game design studios. Since 2008, Alex has been veering back toward illustration, having landed concept art commisions on two feature films currently in production from Black Camel Pictures, the horror combat thriller *Outpost 2* and vampire revenge flick *Blood Makes Noise*.

Lynsey Hutchinson is an illustrator and musician from Edinburgh. When not playing ball-shaking drums in sleazy blues bands or restoring antique surgical instruments, she is the co-creator, writer and artist on the graphic novel *Sceptic: A Magician Among the Spirits*, described as a cross between *Inspector McLevy*, *Hellblazer* and *Deadwood*.

David Alexander was born and dragged up in Glasgow in a strange, frightening time before computers, Photoshop and mobile phones. After serving an apprenticeship in bookbinding he went on to study technical graphics at Glasgow College of Printing. He co-founded *Electric Soup*, the Glasgow adult humour comic in 1989 where his cartoon characters *The MacBam Brothers* made their debut, going on to appear in their own comic in 1994 and the underground title *Northern Lightz* in 1999. His work has also appeared in *Ganjaman Presents*, *Wasted* and under the pseudonym HobNob he currently contributes to *VIZ* magazine, with his brilliant scriptwriter Biscuit Tin.

Stuart Beel actually started working on *Burke & Hare* in the mid-1990s when he was young, crap and irresponsible. Now he's OLD crap and irresponsible and cannot apologise to Martin enough. In-between then and now many fools have taken him on-board as an in-house creative type doing doodles of characters and environments, and what not. He apologises to Martin for dicking him about, but now lives in Edinburgh and is of Irish desent.

PJ Holden is a Belfast based comic artist. His work has been published by *2000AD*, Image Comics, Dynamite Entertainment, Fantagraphics and Games Workshop. His website can be found at www.pauljholden.com

Stephen Daly was born in Dublin, Ireland. He trained as an animator before turning to work in feature films and TV. He has worked extensively as a production designer, art director and storyboard artist. Comics have been a lifelong love of his ever since his father bought him a copy *The Amazing Spider-Man* back in 1977. The comic is long gone, but its effect remains...

Stephen White lives in Edinburgh and works under the pen-name 'Stref'. He started his career working for The City Of Edinburgh Council as in-house illustrator back in 1987. Since then, he has worked on weekly commissions for DC Thomson's comic publications, *The Dandy* and *The Beano*. The main strips he contributed to include *Winker Watson*, *Dennis the Menace* and *The Bash Street Kids*. Stephen's first graphic novel, *Milk* was published in September 2009 - a project that he worked on for many years in his spare time.

Hugh Parker is an architect who never quite got over his first love - comic art. He first worked with Martin Conaghan in the early 90s on a story called *Pendulum* for a short-lived, independently published anthology title, and went on to illustrate character sketches for other stories. He has been practising as an architect for nearly 15 years and, now that he has almost got it right, is dabbling again in comic art. He lives in London with his wife and their two children, whose incessant demands for superhero drawings have hastened his return.

Gary Erskine currently lives in Glasgow, Scotland. He has been illustrating for twenty years and contributed character designs and storyboards for television, commercials and games development working with various companies including DC and Marvel Comics, Dark Horse, Virgin Comics, Titan Books and Panini. He has collaborated on *The Filth* with Grant Morrison and Chris Weston and most recently re-envisioned *Dan Dare* with Garth Ennis. His varied career has also included work on licensed properties such as *Star Wars*, *Terminator*, *The Mask* and Dreamworks characters (including *Shrek* and *Madagascar*).

Frank Quitely is the award-winning artist of DC Comics' *All Star Superman* and the Vertigo mini-series *We3*. His first published work appeared in the Glasgow humour comic *Electric Soup*, before moving on to *Shimura* in the *Judge Dredd Megazine*, *The Authority* for DC Wildstorm, *Flex Mentallo* for DC Vertigo and *New X-Men* for Marvel Comics. He recently worked on the series *Batman & Robin* with regular collaborator Grant Morrison for DC.

BIOGRAPHIES AND ACKNOWLEDGEMENTS

Martin Conaghan's first published writing work appeared in Aceville Publications' *Comic World* in 1992, which was followed by work for *2000AD* and Caliber Comics. During the late 1990s he moved into mainstream journalism, producing a weekly internet column for *The Big Issue* and has written for every major Scottish newspaper. From 1999, he worked in sports broadcasting for the BBC and now works as an award-winning producer-director on television documentaries and investigations. In 2011, he won Best Writer and Best Graphic Novel for *Burke & Hare* at the Scottish Independent Comic Book Awards.

Will Pickering has been drawing comics intermittently since the age of two. His work appeared in various small press titles in the 1990s, including his self-published supervillain series *Something Fast*. Following stints as a music journalist, youth worker, marketing executive and community activist, he returned to the medium in 2008 with *The Spectacular Santa Claus*, and began work on *Burke & Hare* soon after. Subsequent swork has appeared in several anthologies and he is the regular artist on Planet Jimbot's *Wolf Country*.

ACKNOWLEDGEMENTS

Martin would like to thank: the staff of Coatbridge Library for an extended loan of their books, the staff at the National Library in Edinburgh, Sheena Robb, Dr Gordon Findlater at the University of Edinburgh Medical Faculty, Professor Matthew Kaufman, John McShane, Stuart Beel, Neil Hood, Vincent Deighan, Gary Erskine, Dave Alexander, Stephen Daly, Alex Ronald, Lynsey Hutchinson, Paul McLaren, Rich Johnston, Richard Johnson, Stephen Donnelly, Julie Broadfoot, Thomas McGuigan - and my good friend Dave Hill. Also, special thanks are due to the late Gary Reed and to Joe Pruett for starting me off on the Burke and Hare quest, to Nic Wilkinson and Alasdair Duncan, to Alan Grant for his invaluable introduction, Rian Hughes at Device for his two captivating covers - and, to my wife Susan, as ever, for listening. Of course, thanks to Will for taking on an extraordinary burden of effort in breathing life to my humble script.

Will would like to thank: the many contemporary and near-contemporary artists whose outstanding preparatory work made the resurrection of nineteenth century Edinburgh a viable proposition in the first place, including Sirs David Wilkie, Henry Raeburn and George Watson Gordon, the Faed brothers, JMW Turner, George Cottermole, James Skene, John Wilson Ewbank, Jane Stewart Smith, David Octavius Hill and others, but above all the mighty, mighty, Thomas Hosmer Shepherd (may his name be praised). Thanks also to Hamish Horsburgh, Peter Stubbs, Julie Bennet and Sir Tim Berners-Lee for saving legwork, and to Imogen Gibbon at the National Portrait Gallery and the staffs of Surgeons' Hall, Central Library and the Edinburgh Police Museum for their help on the ground; with special thanks to Lynsey, middlewoman extraordinaire.

ALSO AVAILABLE FROM CALIBER COMICS

QUALITY GRAPHIC NOVELS TO ENTERTAIN

THE SEARCHERS: VOLUME 1
The Shape of Things to Come

Before *League of Extraordinary Gentlemen* there was *The Searchers*. At the dawn of the 20th Century the greatest literary adventurers from the minds of Wells, Doyle, Burroughs, and Haggard were created. All thought to be the work of pure fiction. However, a century later, the real-life descendents of those famous characters are recuited by the legendary Professor Challenger in order to save mankind's future. Series collected for the first time.

"Searchers is the comic book I have on the wall with a sign reading - 'Love books? Never read a comic? Try this one! ....money back guarantee..." - Dark Star Books.

WAR OF THE WORLDS: INFESTATION

Based on the H.G. Wells classic! The "Martian Invasion" has begun again and now mankind must fight for its very humanity. It happened slowly at first but by the third year, it seemed that the war was almost over... the war was almost lost.

"Writer Randy Zimmerman has a fine grasp of drama, and spins the various strands of the story into a coherent whole... imaginative and very gritty."
- war-of-the-worlds.co.uk

HELSING: LEGACY BORN

From writer Gary Reed (Deadworld) and artists John Lowe (Captain America), Bruce McCorkindale (Godzilla). She was born into a legacy she wanted no part of and pushed into a battle recessed deep in the shadows of the night. Samantha Helsing is torn between two worlds...two allegiances...two families. The legacy of the Van Helsing family and their crusade against the "night creatures" comes to modern day with the most unlikely of all warriors.

"Congratulations on this masterpiece..."
- Paul Dale Roberts, Compuserve Reviews

"All in all, another great package from Caliber."
- Paul Haywood, Comics Forum

DEADWORLD

Before there was The Walking Dead there was Deadworld. Here is an introduction of the long running classic horror series, Deadworld, to a new audience! Considered by many to be the godfather of the original zombie comic with over 100 issues and graphic novels in print and over 1,000,000 copies sold, Deadworld ripped into the undead with intelligent zombies on a mission and a group of poor teens riding in a school bus desperately try to stay one step ahead of the sadistic, Harley-riding King Zombie. Death, mayhem, and a touch of supernatural evil made Deadworld a classic and now here's your chance to get into the story!

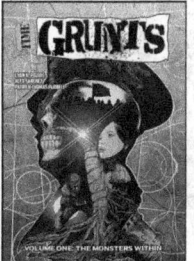

DAYS OF WRATH

Award winning comic writer & artist Wayne Vansant brings his gripping World War II saga of war in the Pacific to Guadalcanal and the Battle of Bloody Ridge. This is the powerful story of the long, vicious battle for Guadalcanal that occurred in 1942-43. When the U.S. Navy orders its outnumbered and outgunned ships to run from the Japanese fleet, they abandon American troops on a bloody, battered island in the South Pacific.

"Heavy on authenticity, compellingly written and beautifully drawn."
- Comics Buyers Guide

THE BOBCAT

Described as the Native American *Black Panther*. 1898. Indian Territory. Will Firemaker is a Cherokee Blacksmith who is finding out that the world of ancient lore and myth of his Tribe, that Will had always thought of as tribal fairytales, are actually true, and they're telling him he must replace his best friend from the animal kingdom, The Great Cat, as the guardian of his people. This sends him down a path of shock and disbelief as beings from the ancient past begin to manifest themselves in the world of reality. And as malevolent forces rise up in the wake of the fledgling Industrial Age, the future rushes head on into the Old West. Tahlequah will never be the same...

TIME GRUNTS

What if Hitler's last great Super Weapon was – Time itself! A WWII/time travel adventure that can best be described as Band of Brothers meets Time Bandits.

October, 1944. Nazi fortunes appear bleaker by the day. But in the bowels of the Wenceslas Mines, a terrible threat has emerged . . . The Nazis have discovered the ability to conquer time itself with the help of a new ominous device!

Now a rag tag group of American GIs must stop this threat to the past, present, and future . . . While dealing with their own past, prejudices, and fears in the process.

LEGENDLORE

From Caliber Comics now comes the entire Realm and Legendlore saga as a set of volumes that collects the long running critically acclaimed series. In the vein of The Lord of The Rings and The Hobbit with elements of Game of Thrones and Dungeon and Dragons.

Four normal modern day teenagers are plunged into a world they thought only existed in novels and film. They are whisked away to a magical land where dragons roam the skies, orcs and hobgoblins terrorize travelers, where unicorns prance through the forest, and kingdoms wage war for dominance. It is a world where man is just one race, joining other races such as elves, trolls, dwarves, changelings, and the dreaded night creatures who steal the night.

CALIBER
COMICS

www.calibercomics.com

CPSIA information can be obtained
at www.ICGtesting.com
Printed in the USA
BVHW012235120322
631351BV00013B/772